BEST PRACTICES FOR
GRAPHIC DESIGNERS: PACKAGING

© 2013 ROCKPORT PUBLISHERS

FIRST PUBLISHED IN THE UNITED STATES OF AMERICA IN 2013 BY
Rockport Publishers, a member of Quayside Publishing Group
100 Cummings Center
Suite 406-L
Beverly, Massachusetts 01915-6101

TELEPHONE: (978) 282-9590
FAX: (978) 283-2742
WWW.ROCKPUB.COM
VISIT ROCKPAPERINK.COM TO SHARE YOUR OPINIONS, CREATIONS, AND PASSION
FOR DESIGN.

LIBRARY OF CONGRESS CATALOGING-IN-PUBLICATION DATA
ISBN: 978-1-59253-813-3
DIGITAL EDITION PUBLISHED IN 2013
EISBN: 978-1-61058-952-9

10 9 8 7 6 5 4 3 2 1

DESIGN: GRIP

PRINTED IN CHINA

BEST PRACTICES FOR
GRAPHIC DESIGNERS: PACKAGING

AN ESSENTIAL GUIDE
FOR IMPLEMENTING EFFECTIVE
PACKAGE DESIGN SOLUTIONS

GRIP X CHICAGO

Rockport Publishers
100 Cummings Center, Suite 406L
Beverly, MA 01915

rockpub.com • rockpaperink.com

CONTENTS

A nother book on package design? This one is different, we promise. This book is about all the lessons we've learned in over a decade of experience designing a wide variety of packages. But this is also about our peers, the designers and strategists who create thoughtful packaging solutions with style, panache, and ingenuity in engineering. We wrote this book because we're passionate about this part of our studio practice and we're continually inspired by the work being done in this sector of our industry. We see this book as a resource for young designers or for veterans looking to expand their expertise. And, of course, we are thrilled to feature some of our favorite clients and many of our admired colleagues.

Package design is perhaps the most evolutionary corner of the entire design industry. While most disciplines swing to the ebb and flow of trending color, type, styles, etc., package design has a literal and figurative z-axis that is the physical form itself. Combined with rapid advancements in materials, and a greater understanding of the psychology of purchasing, we could argue that packaging is the most engaging and challenging work out there for designers.

On the following pages you will find curated project case studies with behind-the-scenes anecdotes, technical details, perspectives from different designers and vendors, and lessons learned. (Ahem, there's also a lot be learned from packaging mishaps or unforeseen obstacles in manufacturing. We've included these stories as well, with a few words of advice, in hopes that you will avoid the same costly mistakes.)

While we certainly won't claim this to be the definitive guide for package design, this book intends to put some real case studies before you that solve real-world problems. We hope you find the book resourceful, entertaining, inspiring and, duh, well-designed. Let's get started!

Chapter 1
SHELVING, DESIGNED TO SELL

It is easy to kick back in the rarified air at your computer screen and dream up fantastic package designs. Then it happens. The product goes to production, gets loaded onto pallets, and somewhere an underpaid kid grabs your hard work and throws it onto a shelf. Sideways. Of course, it doesn't always happen like this, but accommodating imperfect circumstances is one of the most important considerations when designing for the shelf.

• • •

Target is well known for a process known as "merchandising in multiples" and the psychology behind it. Essentially, a large rack with many of the same item conveys not only newness (freshness in the case of giant stacks of produce), but also provides a giant billboard for the product. Increasing the ease of quick purchasing decisions is one key to improving sales. Think about how many times you have been reminded that you are out of detergent when faced with a large display, conveniently located at whatever height you are because the *entire* shelf is a single product. Target has the luxury of large amounts of real estate that most other retailers do not, unfortunately. What you design needs to convey the brand promise and function quickly, and with a single unit. No small task.

Another consideration that designers typically overlook is the "pay-to-play" nature of marketing on store shelves. In its most basic form (and there are many, many iterations of how products get placed and how much it costs) a company will pay by the linear foot for premium shelf placement. Small, outward-facing packages with increased depth tend to fare very well in paid environments. The soft drink twelve-pack is a prime example of how to take advantage of shelf depth while minimizing linear feet.

Unique form factors are also critical for differentiation among commodity products. Even saying "bag of Pringles" sounds wrong. In fact, that package is so unique to the category that most people reference it only by product name without mention of the carrier. Rather than spread throughout the chip section, they tend to be stocked in their own area, further reinforcing how a package can establish a brand.

Now we have arrived at the moment of truth: the package is designed, production run complete, the pick, pack, ship, and stock have all gone down. There on the shelf sits your finest work. But will anyone buy it? A best practice we regularly employ prior to this moment is to comp and—we can't officially recommend this— either through professional channels, friends who own stores, or just guerrilla-style, stock a shelf with fake product.

Why go through all this? Because the psychology of purchasing is very complex and nothing beats having a little ethnographic research, however small the sample size. Do people stop?

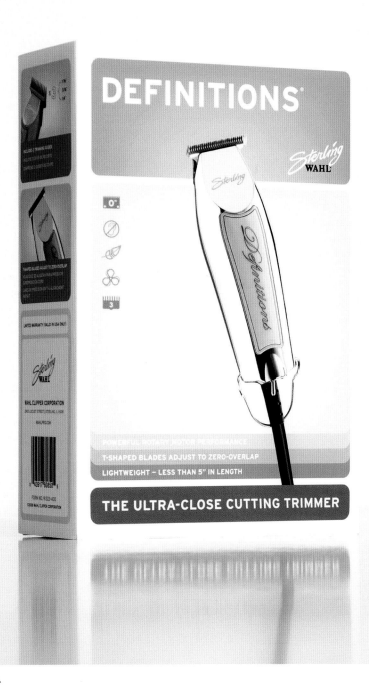

WAHL CLIPPER
Grip, USA

PROJECT DESCRIPTION & DESIGN STRATEGY:

Wahl has provided the beauty and barber industry with innovative, high-quality clippers and trimmers since 1919. The current marketplace of packaging in this industry is chock full of bright color and information overload for product features.

A staple among professional stylists, Wahl products have had the luxury of outstanding name recognition. Taking cues from high-end cosmetic and fragrance packaging, the approved concept employed a limited color palette of blue, gray, and black. The near-monochromatic and simplified visuals provide breathing room on the shelf and easily draw the eye from the competition, particularly when placed in multiples.

LESSONS LEARNED ALONG THE WAY:

Highly reflective products can be a challenge to photograph properly. Retouching may involve removal of any object in the room during the shoot. Wahl products were in some cases rendered realistically (in part or in whole) to eliminate extensive retouching. What seems like a simple table-top shoot, can be terribly difficult depending on the reflectiveness of the subject matter.

The redesigned Wahl packaging employs plenty of negative space to highlight the product first and foremost. Features are showcased smaller, giving the hero shot top billing on each box.

Monochromatic packaging from Wahl dominate retail displays, especially in multiples. The clipper market is currently saturated with bright colors and feature-heavy packaging.

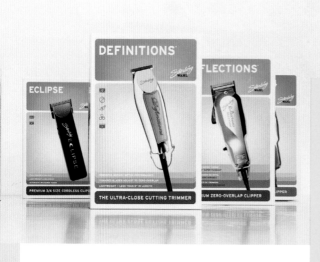

TIP

Chrome product photography can be shot incorporating large panels to block out reflections in the studio, or in a white photobooth, particularly for hand-held products. Hyper-realistic renderings can be used in whole or in part to compensate for difficult substrates. Or, build time into your deadline schedule to hire a professional photographer who specializes in shooting reflective products.

Studies show that if you can motivate someone to pick up the product, purchasing conversions increase dramatically. But what can you do to encourage this?

While every product category is different, there are two major components that time and time again seem to influence behavior: Typography and Texture. Most of us, having spent years setting type for different industries, recognize how to make something appear expensive, cheap, humorous, or even rebellious, using only type.

Remember the typeface Crackhouse? We wish we didn't, but that doesn't mean that it didn't convey "crazy and irreverent" for thousands of packages. Usually Halloween costumes.

The same urgency can be applied to packaging that either has its own tactility or leverages the distinct qualities of the product it contains. It is for this reason alone that Koosh Balls have little more than some cardboard for brand messaging and rack merchandising. The texture begs you to touch, if not pick it up, and picking up a product is one giant leap toward purchasing.

The package should reflect the needs of the end user. This should be second nature, but we see so many packages and portfolios that contain wildly inappropriate aesthetics that more often than not reflect the taste level of the designer and not the potential customer.

On occasion you may want to intentionally deviate from this rule, but understanding the significance of who will be interested in the product can never be overstated. One acceptable deviation from this rule of thumb is when trying to elevate a commodity product into an aspirational one. When grocery stores redesign their house labels to mimic the more expensive brands that outperform their products is a good example of recognizing that some purchasing decisions are driven by refined design.

Quite often, however, the form factor of a package is pre-determined by your client before alternatives may even be considered. In our work with Wahl, we could affect only the cardboard sleeve that wrapped the outside. Given that most consumers prefer to actually see the merchandise, and a clear window was beyond the scope of production, our direction was set.

SUPERGOOP

Design Packaging Inc., USA

PROJECT DESCRIPTION & DESIGN STRATEGY:

The concept behind the slanted, top-folding box was to maximize the waist-level shelving real estate of the product. By determining the proper slant angle, the normally less-than-prime shelf space is color-blocked by SuperGoop. The structure increased visibility at varying distances and, coupled with the bright lid colors, created a unified billboard space.

The terry-cloth tote gift-with-purchase item that became a staple product was designed to be an easy way to carry product to and from the beach or pool, but also serve as a wet-bikini or toddler-suit carrier to keep all of your dry goods dry. The concept of on-brand reusability came together with the terry tote both structurally and functionally.

LESSONS LEARNED ALONG THE WAY:

Creating unusual angles in packaging requires the ability to think through both production methods and packaging logistics. Due to the angles, the flat pack initially had extra flaps that added to the flattened box's footprint, increasing shipping and storage requirements. Through several rounds of production fine-tuning, all the loose ends were eliminated and the flattened box's final footprint was optimized for shipping and storage.

TIP

The box's locking tuck flap, given the lid angle, made the box impenetrable without destroying the lid. As a security feature this is a plus, but as a restocking feature, it's a nightmare. Damaged boxes could not be restocked, so locking tuck flaps were replaced with friction-fit flaps to allow opening and restocking.

TIP

For international packaging, a consideration that goes into each and every pack is where does that "Country of Origin (COO)" go? If you are importing anything, your COO must be on the pack, and if there is any address printed on the pack, the COO must go below it in the same font, color, and size.

DEATH'S DOOR SPIRITS

Grip, USA

PROJECT DESCRIPTION & DESIGN STRATEGY:

With the deeply collaborative nature of our relationship with Death's Door Spirits—we are both the agency of record AND shareholders—we were able to impact shelf presence to a greater degree. This case study illustrates some of the difficulties that occur when our work leaves the monitor and enters the real world.

The original concepts for Death's Door Gin & Vodka focused on the story of Washington Island wheat farmers, and the fact that Death's Door intended to revive its struggling agriculture by producing spirits from its hard red wheat. However, in our first iterations of the packaging, the story was not succinct or obvious to the potential buyer. After much consideration and reflection, we collectively felt the wheat-focused illustrations did not accurately tell the story, nor did they differentiate the product. The approved direction focused on the care, quality, and craftsmanship of each spirit while still giving visual clues to its mission of sustainability.

Sales materials indicated how the bottles were to be strategically located on store shelves (a bold move considering Death's Door was a fairly new product among a long list of established veterans). Vendors followed those guidelines—much to the delight of Death's Door—and the spirit garnered premium placement alongside more established high-end brands. Sales more than quadrupled following the redesign and new sales materials.

TIP

Always check box sizes and ensure fitting of necessary product separators—and test the prototype with the exact product that should fit snugly and safely inside. Remember, glass production is not an exact science, so a little wiggle room is important, but not so much that you're putting the product at risk during shipping.

Without having enough samples to test a proposed case stacker dieline, the first box was too tight to properly fit the number of bottles needed—a mistake we corrected with the second run of the cases.

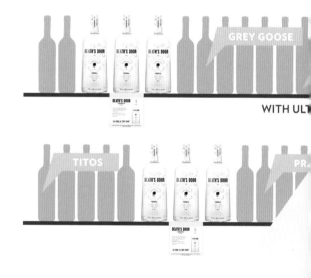

WILD OPHELIA

(a division of Vosges Haut-Chocolat)

Wink Design Atelier, USA

PROJECT DESCRIPTION & DESIGN STRATEGY:

Wild Ophelia is the wilder, more vocal, younger sister brand to Vosges Haut-Chocolat. The concept behind the brand is a journey or road trip exploring America's esteemed farms and foods such as beef jerky, barbecue, and cherry pie. To portray the more amplified flavors and artisanal qualities than its older sister brand, bright fluorescent colors were selected and the type was hand drawn.

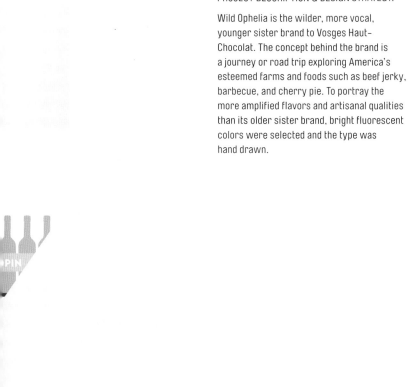

TIP

The designer, Brenda Rotheiser Bergen, says, "Be sure you insist on a press check. Unfortunately, the print job on the first run of these boxes was off register with the embossing. The next run of these boxes will be much better."

Chapter 2

BEYOND THE SHELF, DESIGNING FOR USAGE

TO INFINITY. Beyond protecting and merchandising a product, what is left for a package to accomplish? In a word: everything. At every step, we challenge ourselves to consider the life of both the materials and the possible reuse of the package itself.

• • •

Y ou will hear us say many times over that while recycling is fantastic, the best a package can do is maintain utility through reuse. Anytime that occurs, one less landfill is created, one less product is purchased (yes, this is a good thing), and hopefully we can avoid creating another toxic, plastic floating island.

Editorial note: While we recognize the inherent waste that comes with most packaging and our role in this, we feel a grave responsibility to use what power we have to steer clients into thoughtful decisions about the role their packaging plays for future generations. If you haven't seen it already, we highly encourage viewing Vice magazine's excellent video on the effect of negligent plastic disposal: www.gripdesign.com/packaging/waste/.

We have recently witnessed everything from designer chairs cut and composed of corrugated cardboard (priced, shall we say, Not Within Reach), to cardboard boxes with illustrated directions explaining how to construct a shelter. With the advent of increasingly complex dies and tools like laser cutting, there has never been a greater time to consider not just the package and its contents, but how they can be repurposed. To achieve this, we recommend working through your standard design process, but before finalizing production specs,

take a moment and write down what each component of the package could do when thought of as a raw material.

From milk jugs with printed lines to cut and become dustpans, to used lotion bottles repurposed into beach-friendly phone and money containers, the possibility for life after delivery is endless. To jump-start your creative process, search "best life hacks" and get ready to lose a couple of hours.

Without getting too "Star-Trek-y" we would love to live in a world where the things we purchase can be re-created into other things we need. The advent of 3D printers has opened up myriad possibilities. Consider that when you have finished a bottle of orange juice, the plastic can be fed into a machine that would subsequently shred, heat, and then form the shape of a different item. We live in a world of finite resources, and recognizing this is part of becoming a great designer. As with aesthetic decisions, every choice matters when speccing a new project. The initial phases of package development are the easiest time to set goals and standards for environmental impact when the job is finished. Be creative, have fun, and never be afraid to present a client with a bold new approach to life beyond their product's trip home.

BRUKETA & ŽINIĆ, CROATIA
Brokula & Ž

PROJECT DESCRIPTION & DESIGN STRATEGY:

Brokula & Ž (Broccoli & Ž) is a clothing brand by Bruketa & Žinić OM, made from organically grown materials. Brokula & Ž believes everything good comes from within, so all of the clothing contains hidden messages written on the inside that can be seen only by you...and whoever undresses you. The messages are actually funny dialogues between Brokula (Broccoli) and Ž (a bird), who are the main characters of the product's visual identity. Like the products themselves, the packaging is also eco-friendly and was designed to be easy to assemble, without any glue or plastic. The inks have ecological certificates, and the paper is recycled. Furthermore, the packaging is designed as a cup that you can use for something else after unpacking your purchase.

TIP

The packaging had to be as eco-friendly as possible to align with the product and accurately represent the company's commitment to sustainability. When the packaging feels like an extension of the product, it adds value. In this case, the packaging serves many purposes, from emotional to tactical. In addition to the ecological considerations, the packaging has to serve as a fun gift wrap and a practical protection of the product.

BOOKJIGS
Modern8, USA

PROJECT DESCRIPTION & DESIGN STRATEGY:

Bookjigs is an original product innovation for a common need—bookmarks that attach to your book and include a ribbon so you never lose your place. Modern8 was originally engaged to design just the packaging but convinced the client that they should create an integrated approach by simultaneously designing both the product graphics and the package. They designed five different themes with six products in each theme. The corresponding countertop displays are not only aesthetically charming but also incredibly effective by showcasing how the product works.

TIP

Wrapping the ribbon outside of the packaging proved to be somewhat of a headache for the designers as well as the client. Thankfully the idea was well supported, and the client was patient and excited enough to see the design achieved as intended. In the end, headaches and all, everyone involved was very happy with the result.

BUTTER! BETTER!
Yeongkeun Jeong, USA

PROJECT DESCRIPTION & DESIGN STRATEGY:

This project came about through a genuine "a-ha" moment. The designer was enjoying a picnic lunch with friends and realized she'd forgotten to pack a knife with which to spread the butter. After laugh-worthy attempts to spread butter using the floppy foil lid, she imagined a simple remedy with a small change to the lid of the butter packet. Modernizing such a ubiquitous item ultimately enhances and changes an everyday food—bread and butter—making it simpler, smarter, and more special.

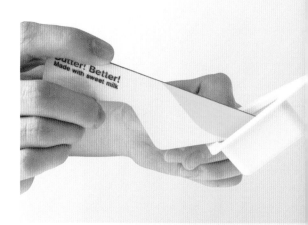

TIP

The ultimate goal in packaging is to achieve something that is both functional and beautiful. Don't overlook even the smallest of everyday problems, like needing a utensil to spread butter. This package is highly functional and convenient for users and solves the problem in a simple, unexpected way. This solution, particularly because it is a food item, involves all of the senses and enhances the experience of using the product.

Till Open

TOSHIBA

THE PEOPLE SUPERMARKET

For the people, by the people

LAMB'S CONDUIT ST. LONDON

Chapter 3

WORKING WITH A BUDGET

BUDGET ABOUT IT. We have all heard the pitch. It goes something like this: "We really want to work with you guys on this, but it cost so much just to get to this point that we just don't have the budget for expensive packaging." Sound familiar? There was a time that this type of project would seriously grate on our creative mojo. After a while, however, we learned to embrace the limitations of constrictive production budgets and instead push the boundaries of what is possible with fewer colors, preproduced boxes, and nontraditional or repurposed packaging vehicles.

•••

Today, when we see someone create meaningful packaging with very little cost, we are envious. It is easy to appreciate a custom glass bottle with twelve-color printing, but a standard stock bottle with amazing typography on a simple label can be just as effective, and beautiful.

This brings us to the single most important aspect of budget design: typography. Type is necessary, type is cheap, and type can convey legions about the product positioning. We have done one-color case design with nothing more than a small illustration of a map and loads of carefully set type. To this day, that design stands out in the market, and we continue our relationship with the company.

One of our favorite budget tricks is to look for neutral, midtone base materials for package design. A great midtone allows two-color jobs to appear as three colors and allows simple black and white to have enough contrast to remain legible.

In some cases, such as clear glass or plastic packaging, the product itself should be considered a color to be worked with and taken advantage of. Of course,

this at times may also be a detriment. We have seen all-natural blood orange soda packaged in clear plastic bottles only to have sunlight degrade the color of the contents to something that would graciously be described as deep tan, but in reality was more akin to a bottle of turds. Even budget packages need to take into account the requirements of the product. One final thought about budgets: Amazing work has been created with next to no money, and complete crap has been created with enormous resources. The sole difference is the amount of thought the designer put into the process, and last we checked, thinking was free.

TIP

No matter your client's budget, always invoice new clients 50 percent before any work begins—no matter how nice they may be. As a company you need to retain some leverage (e.g., holding on to final files) until the bill is paid. The law is not on the side of the designer when it comes to getting paid. This is particularly important for packaging projects, because you often buy samples during the design phase, as well as materials and supplies before and during the production process. Those costs shouldn't be out of pocket for the design firm.

THE PEOPLE'S SUPERMARKET
Unreal, UK

PROJECT DESCRIPTION & DESIGN STRATEGY:

The People's Supermarket is a community-based shop managed by its members and open to all. Unreal developed the brand and identity to reflect the co-op's core values: affordability, community, and democracy.

TIP

For clients with smaller budgets, the production budget should form part of the initial brief. The solution for The People's Supermarket was to create branded sleeves and stickers that could be used in conjunction with existing generic packaging. This provided a low-cost solution for branding and packaging.

BRAND
GUIDELINES

ARTHUR POTTS-DAWSON
Founder Member

(0207) 4040924
72 - 78 LAMB'S CONDUIT ST.
LONDON WC1N 3LP
INFO@PEOPLESSUPERMARKET.ORG
THEPEOPLESSUPERMARKET.ORG

THE PEOPLE'S
SUPERMARKET

For the people, by the people

LAMB'S CONDUIT ST. LONDON

ONE VILLAGE COFFEE
Able Design, USA

PROJECT DESCRIPTION & DESIGN STRATEGY:

One Village Coffee (OVC) is a specialty roaster located outside Philadelphia. Their goal when they opened three years ago was to direct some of their profits to nonprofit partners in a small village in Nigeria. Since then, they have helped organizations around the world on various levels of development work, including a deworming project for children in Honduras and educational development in several parts of Nigeria.

The designers spent a couple days riding along with the sales team and watched them interact with coffee shop owners. The sales team was greeted like friends, not vendors. They sat and drank espresso, talked business, coffee, and even family. They watched them hang with the crew at Whole Foods as if they had been friends since grade school. Designer Greg Ash says, "It was remarkable. At the end of those interactions we realized that the word village is just another word for relationship—friend, cousin, homey, clique, fraternity, club. One Village Coffee is people with other people. The whole premise behind One Village is an open invitation for people to come together. We recognize the power of the masses, and as we used to say as kids, 'Two is more fun than one.'"

It is always a challenge to translate the knowledge from real life into tactile and representational design. "We knew there would be a lot of people that would be interacting with the bag, so we needed to

try and capture that diversity," Ash explains. Prior to this bag, the packaging had been mostly a maroon color. Making the shift to maroon + blue was a difficult decision. There were a lot of unknowns, including uncertainty that customers would recognize the new brand. The brand wants to appeal to a more youthful demographic and increase its shelf presence to transition out of the local craft roaster and into a regional specialty roaster category.

There's only one version of the new package, making it more economical. Labels are added to the bag to denote the roast and flavor profile.

GLO
Rule29 Creative, USA

PROJECT DESCRIPTION & DESIGN STRATEGY:

Glo is an interactive Bible that brings the book to life through five main lenses: high-definition video, photography, maps, reading plans, and 360-degree virtual tours—all with a unique zoomable interface for fast, easy visual navigation. Rule29 designed the main product packaging, as well as various in-store displays, all within a modest budget. A contemporary and colorful style was applied to achieve a sense of quality and vitality in the product, without adding to the production budget.

TIP

Doing an off-the-shelf box for a conservative market is challenging because they aren't created very often, if at all anymore. The design team had to create a memorable package that was as cost-effective as possible. To do this, they met early and often with the manufacturers and vendors to create prototypes until they found the most effective use of the paper stock and the production costs.

HARRIET'S JOLLY NICE ICE CREAM

Taxi Studio, Ltd., UK

PROJECT DESCRIPTION & DESIGN STRATEGY:

According to the design firm Taxi Studio, their client Harriet Wilson makes the world's greatest ice cream. What could be more fun to package? But printing on clear tubs was more problematic than originally imagined, largely because they specified each package (there were six in total) to have four unique Pantone colors plus black and white (which were common among all). This resulted in a print run of twenty-two colors in total...and the client could only afford six. New plan: Switch everything to CMYK plus white and black. Some colors were trickier to reproduce using process colors, and Taxi boosted the intensity of most colors, especially since the substrate is clear. They also thickened the type considerably to compensate for both the process registration and the transparency of the plastic tub.

TIP

When your project assignment is to package Salted Caramel Ice Cream, ask for many, many samples. For creative inspiration, of course.

42

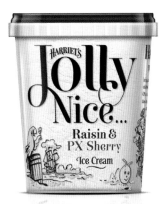

CREMA NUTRITIVA
DE CAVIAR
CON EXTRACTO
Y ALOE VERA
50ML

greenpharma

CREMA
REAFIRMANTE 24 H
BABA DE CARACOL
Y ALOE VERA
FPS 15
50ML

CREMA
VENENO DE
SERPIENTE
50ML

greenpharma

...AGE
RESPLANDOR
BABA DE CARACOL,
ALOE VERA
Y ROSA MOSQUETA
FPS 15
50ML

greenpharma

CREMA
VINO Y ALOE
50ML

greenpharma

CREMA
REVITALIZANTE
CON EXTRACTO DE
ESTRELLA DE MAR,
CRISALIDA DE SEDA
Y AGUA TERMAL
FPS 15
50ML

greenpharma

GEL INTENSIVO
BORRADOR DE
ARRUGAS
EFECTO BOTOX
50ML

greenpharma

CF
RE
CC
VE
MC
50

greenp

Chapter 4

NAMING SYSTEMS + VARIETIES

MAKING THE MOST OF MULTIPLES. If you work in package design for any length of time, at some point you will be required to solve the problems associated with multiproduct brand families. For example, a coffee company may have one bag, but several varietals that need to be distinguishable from one another. It goes without saying that, in general, it is best to remain consistent with your typography and basic image treatments to maintain cohesion throughout the line. But this is also the perfect opportunity to select a color system that can accommodate a wide range of line extensions while still coordinating when merchandised side-by-side. Here's the real challenge: finding the balance between cohesion along the product line and enough differentiation that each item has its own character.

• • •

One of our clients is a fantastic craft beer company with a serious love of seasonality among its product line. As such, there is a tremendous amount of turnover when new flavor profiles are appropriate for the weather, harvest, or mood of the brewmaster. After establishing image guidelines and determining that the typography could support variation between labels, we created a chart that showed the complete color family and how various combinations could drive the brand extensions for years to come. *See the Arcadia Ales case study on page 91.*

Bear in mind that when you are faced with a multiproduct project, creating expensive custom packaging is not the only avenue to success. Material sourcing stock items can also be a very good method of creating unity. One of our favorite examples of clever—and highly marketable—design is on display with a pickle company named Rick's Picks (rickspicksnyc.com). Utilizing materials that could have been purchased from a grocery store and a label that could be produced from any home inkjet printer, the brand has a strong sense of identity along the entire line. Further, when the company needed a more traditional pickle jar, the aesthetic carried over seamlessly. Great ideas do not necessarily require great budgets. An adept eye for typography, imagination with utilizing stock items, and an appealing color palette can yield amazing results. Our only complaint about Rick's Picks is when there's none in our fridge.

DISCOVERING ALTERNATIVE SOLUTIONS. Never underestimate your value to a client when making suggestions about how a family of products can come together. One of the great strengths designers possess is the ability to categorize and organize. It's why we love grids, even when we choose to break them. As part of the process when working with multiproduct packages, our designers have made suggestions such as emphasizing unusual elements by playing with scale to differentiate items with similar layouts. We also find that after trying to work with a complex system and staring at the same layout for hours on end, better naming methodologies will pop into our heads organically, because we've been eating, breathing, and sleeping this product line. While we do not advocate ignoring the chosen client direction, we always make a point of showing alternatives that we have discovered during the design phase. If it's a good client, the additional concept is always appreciated and as a result, we build trust and respect.

TIP

When designing a family of products, there should be no more than a 30 to 40 percent variance between products. Any more variance can create disruption of the product family and confuse potential customers. Comp the items in the design phase, set them on a shelf at a distance, and judge for yourself. When building a brand, you must make a calculated effort to stay on message, and when you're crafting a family of products, it's important to have a level of consistency that allows for recognition as a family.

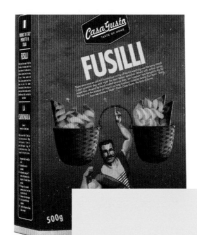

TIP

Packaging doesn't have to be as ho-hum as what's inside the box (or can, or bottle...). Utilize an interesting story—one that is personal to the brand and that speaks to the consumer—to move the product from nondescript to memorable.

CASA GUSTO
The Creative Method, Australia

||||||||||||||||||||||||||||||||||||||||||||||||||||||||||||||||||||||||||||||||||||

PROJECT DESCRIPTION & DESIGN STRATEGY:

The Casa Gusto packaging features images from the Italian Circus in the 1950s, when the owner's father used to travel the country following the circus and sampling the best ingredients. Each package within the Casa Gusto line employs a fun retro aesthetic and shares something personal about the brand. The story told through the series of these packages makes the products feel homemade and authentic and utilizes a quirky sense of humor to cut through the often-bland business of typical bulk food packaging.

BOTANICANUTRIENTS
Grupo Habermas Comunicación, Spain

PROJECT DESCRIPTION & DESIGN STRATEGY:

Botanicadiet, Greenpharma, and Botanicanutrients are designed to convey the natural and healthy ingredients in the products. Each line has its own visual vocabulary with just enough overlap to feel like a well-connected family of products, allowing each grouping of products to leverage the brand equity of the others. The packages balance the look of medical/pharmaceutical aesthetics with the luxury of high-end cosmetics and skin care.

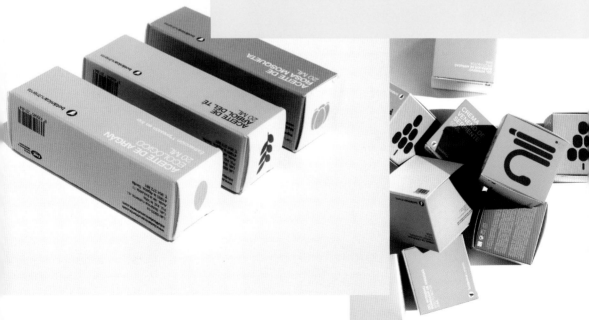

LEVEL GROUND COFFEE

Subplot Design Inc., Canada

PROJECT DESCRIPTION & DESIGN STRATEGY:

Level Ground Trading's mission is to trade fairly and directly with small-scale producers in developing countries, and to market their products in North America, offering their customers ethical choices. As they grew, Level Ground began to compete with more sophisticated brands that were well established, but they stuck to their brand positioning: to celebrate the actual farmers and producers with whom Level Ground maintains direct personal and business relationships. The packaging reinforces this idea that the producer is the real hero, by utilizing intimate, inviting photos of the farmers on the coffee packages.

The unique kraft-covered, zip-lock pouch packs were sourced to combine the best of "authentic, organic, natural" with "resealable freshness." In-depth specs celebrate the coffee origins, from GPS coordinates and elevation, to coffee bean species and harvest months. In addition, a background comprised of weathered paper and actual passport stamps from the owner's passport adds validation and a personal touch.

With each coffee, as well as newly introduced products such as dried fruit and sugar, the brand comes alive consistently with rich variation to tell the whole story of Level Ground and its commitment to fair trade, quality, environmental stewardship, and trade accountability.

TIP

Get real opinions from real consumers. Level Ground Trading conducted focus groups with their customers and learned that the original packaging—slick and metallic—was at odds with the organic, natural origins of the coffee. Even the full-color farmer imagery on the former packages seemed more reminiscent of Oxfam or UNICEF, not a premium roaster of fine coffees. Level Ground listened and redesigned their packaging to reflect their core values as a company, and the products now accurately reflect the brand.

Chapter 5
PRIMARY + SECONDARY PACKAGING

REAL-LIFE TRANSFORMERS. Most packaging requires a multilevel approach to distribution. Typically, a large pallet will be filled with cases of product, which in turn are sold as singular items. The upside of this process is that the package designer is afforded multiple opportunities to convey information. Equally important, we are allowed the opportunity to *omit* information that may be legally required but is of a lesser concern to the individual user. Let's face it, after you have used something half a dozen times, do you really need to be screamed at that the facility where the product was created processes nuts? The big picture is that information is necessary in stages. While we would never advocate that the packaging should underplay the importance of warnings regarding health concerns, we do want to acknowledge that the great majority of products we buy are purchased multiple times and often occupy a part of our lives that exists beyond safety concerns, once we have vetted the integrity of consumption.

• • •

B y now we are all familiar with the "not intended for individual sale" that often accompanies case-packed products. This little bit of lawyer copy is liberating to designers who, ultimately, must satisfy the need for a product to be displayed in an environment as personal as a home or office. Everything from hand soap to honey on some level becomes part of the décor of the room or space they occupy. When considered as "objets d'art," there is not a lot of room for ingredient lists, usage instructions, or lawsuit-protecting legalese. Dial soap made an ease-of-use breakthrough with their foaming hand soap line, but just as important was their decision to let a cardboard sleeve do the heavy lifting of information dissemination while the container itself was kept, pun intended, clean enough to display in a bathroom.

At the end of the day, the most refined environments would prefer to have less branded clutter and more personal attention to detail, and combining the functionality of the foaming soap with an austere form factor was a great way to push design-o-philes into purchasing a disposable product for a room as intimate as a bathroom. We recognize that creating a cardboard sleeve is not exactly primo portfolio material, but in this instance the solution was more about understanding at what point information needs to be conveyed versus how the product will live in an environment.

It is also important to note that providing a disposable vehicle for the required information frees a package designer to highlight interesting techniques in the product itself. Yes, we are blurring the lines between what is a product and what is a package, but the next few years will be defined in part by those "package" designers that can design a package to be as environmentally sensitive as possible. Sometimes this will take the form of adaptive reuse, ease of recycling, as well as minimal material requirements. Designers will be able to take a seat at the table of both product form factor and also the required "wrapping" that works to satisfy the overly litigious environment we must consider when making room available for large amounts of text. After years of attempting to battle with attorneys whose sole function is to achieve absurd levels of legal buffering at the expense of beautiful design, we have learned to accept the ridiculousness of their requests and instead design around the unavoidable onslaught of copy. If you are able to make the mental shift away from their requests ruining your design, and instead provide an easily recyclable/disposable option, the end result can be liberating, beautiful, and an honest expression of your aesthetic intent.

COCA-COLA—TUMULT
Taxi Studio Ltd., UK

||||||||||||||||||||||||||||||||||||||||||||||||||||||||||||||||||||||||||||||

PROJECT DESCRIPTION & DESIGN STRATEGY:

Tumult, owned by Coca-Cola, was perceived as a niche alcohol-free beer-style drink. The challenge was to firmly establish the brand as an iconic adult soft drink with mass appeal. Taxi Studio's internal brief was to set Tumult apart as being the "champagne of soft drinks" or a love child of Fanta and Follador. The new brandmark introduced more dynamism, joy, and personality. The cloud device was retained but dramatically restyled to communicate a more premium, artisan feel—and visually articulate the products' fermented character.

TIP

To achieve the highest possible level of printed detail, Taxi Studio requested a trial print run. They experimented with different levels of color to make sure the swirling dots contrasted beautifully. They also experimented with transparent and opaque inks to allow the metallic nature of the aluminum can to shine through the dots.

GÅNOLA

Jeremy Slagle Graphic Design, USA

PROJECT DESCRIPTION & DESIGN STRATEGY:

Gånola bars are designed for the person who is on the move. Gå is Norwegian for "tread," and their ingredients are 100 percent natural, preservative free, and sweetened with honey and maple syrup. A box was used instead of a wrapper to make each bar stand out from the competition.

TIP

After visiting a local Whole Foods store, the designers did some research on shelf real estate. They brought several of the case boxes with them and noticed some similarities—all were 5.5 inches wide (14cm). Other than that, the depth and height varied among the different brands. They established the size of the bar and relied on the package printer to build a case box based on the client's needs that holds twelve bars and uses the standard 5.5-inch (14cm) width.

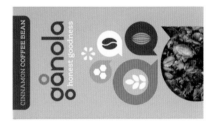

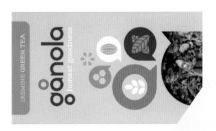

OTO ORGANIC HONEY
Vitrin Studio, Iran

PROJECT DESCRIPTION & DESIGN STRATEGY:

OTO, an organic honey producer, challenged Vitrin Studio to emphasize the natural aspects of the product. An analysis of competitors showed that the current market incorporated dizzying amounts of information on the packaging. Therefore, a more simplistic approach was used to clarify the natural qualities of OTO Organic Honey. Using cardboard in the secondary packaging allowed hexagonal folding to be used. The primary packaging incorporated vintage–shaped labels.

TIP

Sometimes secondary packaging can do the lion's share of product messaging. Honey jars typically allow the product to show through and sell the product. But OTO Organic Honey stands out because of its unexpected shape and simplicity.

COCKTAIL

HAND-CRAFTED MIXER

№ 0

WILLIAMS-SONOMA

Yuzu-Meyer Lemon
FLAVOR

Vodka, Rum, Tequila, Whiskey or
MIX WITH

25.3 fl. oz. (750ml)

ALL-NAT

Chapter 6

IN-HOUSE AGENCIES

BETTER HOUSEKEEPING. If you love challenges, working as an in-house designer is probably one of the most difficult environments you can face. While the benefits of a consistent paycheck, when compared to freelancing, are comforting, the consistent demands of pleasing the same set of clients are daunting. That noted, terrific work is often attributed to small teams who have a tight focus and have "lived" with the same brand and messaging for years. Several luxury brands have very fun in-house teams that over time have learned to play with the borders of their brand standards.

• • •

W illiams-Sonoma has long been on our radar for their consistently excellent packaging of foodstuffs. Perhaps their greatest hallmark is the ability to stay within a branded environment while producing an original aesthetic that appeals to high-net-worth shoppers. This type of shopping profile is drawn to brands with consistent elegance but varied design. The opposite of this type of shopper is the value seeker who finds items merchandised in multiples appealing for their sense of cost-consciousness. For a quick image, think about the way package design and merchandising works in a Walmart versus a Williams-Sonoma. The former has all of the stock exposed for quick identification, while the latter requires the shopper to discover unique items displayed singularly. While the packaging itself is wonderful at converting shoppers, it requires the in-house designer for the respective teams to take on wildly divergent attitudes when creating packaging in each retail setting.

On occasion in-house design teams are asked to develop product lines outside of the standard brand guidelines and need to find a way to "look outside themselves" to differentiate the style of the package or product. Again, the argument of package versus product issues could be discussed, but we are of the ilk that when possible, it is way more fun to consider both, and often that is when minimalist package design is most appropriate.

Consider the work of an in-house communications group. The vast majority of their time is spent on classic marketing channels. One day may be devoted to printed materials and booklets and the next day to online ad development. The truly engaging opportunities really are out there if you actively look for them. In-house design is not dead-end design, but to press your work in new directions, a designer needs to constantly try and find atypical production methods, disruptive marketing messages, and new ways to package it all to sell.

Designer Michael Hester says: "When I began designing, my tendency was to overdesign in the classic Italian style. The result felt too cluttered and not quite right for the internal client. In the end I decided that 'less was more,' and I stripped down the design to strong lines and geographic elements."

WILLIAMS–SONOMA ARTISANAL PASTA
Williams–Sonoma, USA

PROJECT DESCRIPTION & DESIGN STRATEGY:

The Artisanal Pasta collection differentiated itself from the rest of the updated Pantry Essentials product line within the Williams-Sonoma stores. The package needed to reflect the artisanal nature of the heirloom semolina flour used in the pasta. But the packaging was inspired by classic Italian packages. The design solution uses modern architecture references of line, color, and pattern, and still feels artisanal in nature.

Recently we have noticed a growing trend among in-house creatives: embracing the outsourced agency. While not always the case, it should be noted that in-house design teams stand a great deal to gain by allying themselves with a third-party creative team. The trick to executing this is to become the progenitor of the idea to management. When viewed through this lens, an established in-house team can take liberties to slay company-wide sacred cows and "blame" the outside consultants. Some of our recommendations include creating an agenda of what the desired result is, who would need to buy into the process, and how long the relationship should last with a consulting agency. We also advise that the principal in-house members find a way to spend some time out of earshot of management with the leaders of the outsourced team. This may sound counterintuitive to what most people consider design-turf defense, but trust us, the allure of the outside counsel to management is a beautiful siren song that you can utilize to sing your tune.

WILLIAMS–SONOMA COCKTAIL MIXERS
Williams–Sonoma, USA

PROJECT DESCRIPTION & DESIGN STRATEGY:

The concept for these Williams–Sonoma cocktail mixers emulated small–batch whiskey and scotch bottles. The project needed to feel high–end, authentic, and nostalgic. Designer Michael Hester created an intricate level of detail and layering in this line of packaging. The obsessive nature of the design helped communicate the craft put into the product itself, something that proved to be very important to the internal client.

TIP

The right vessel structure and paper stock are key to nailing this concept. A cheap or off-the-shelf solution can make a design look inexpensive or generic.

LAVATORY MISTS
Blue Q, USA

PROJECT DESCRIPTION & DESIGN STRATEGY:

Blue Q decided to create a series of tongue-in-cheek brands to entertain visitors in the lavatory. They sourced very nice, light, upscale scents (so what is in the bottle is as nice as the packaging), and used an apothecary-style bottle that feels solid and old school (even though it's plastic).

The clever copywriting truly gives each package its own voice and language, and the humor is sharp, short, and fresh. The design utilizes mostly pure colors and hip, retro source material. Blue Q then scummed up the artwork for an appealing level of imperfection.

TIP

Never underestimate the power of good copywriting. Mitch Nash, art director and co-owner of Blue Q, says, "This was a writing exercise before it became a visual project, like many things at Blue Q. We love creating products that have comic timing; some say it is our signature trick. For us, the verbal leads to the visual. Writing is key! Our designers have to be funny and embrace working with words and language."

CRAZY BEAUTIFUL WET WIPES

Blue Q, USA

||||||||||||||||||||||||||||||||||||||||||||||||||||||||||||||||||||||||||

PROJECT DESCRIPTION & DESIGN STRATEGY:

The ubiquitous wet wipe needed a packaging makeover, so Blue Q came to the rescue. Wet wipes are a useful item with a great surface area, and Blue Q was confident they would sell in boutiques, gift stores, and grocery stores that carry the Blue Q products.

Blue Q studied the printing and packaging process right from the start; there are many limitations and considerations in package printing, and it's important to understand these before creating mock-ups or artwork. For instance, for the wet wipe packaging, the particular web presses used for printing work in low DPI and have an inherently slightly sloppy quality that the designer—and artwork—needs to anticipate.

Just as Blue Q was starting to think about decorating the wipes, a few illustrious poets visited their offices; they were in town for a spoken-word festival and were hired for a special one-hour performance at the company warehouse. Nash says, "Derrick C. Brown of Austin, Texas, blew us away with his hilarious, brilliant work, and we hired him to write the project. His writing is ambitious yet accessible—different than anything we have ever worked with. We gave him a framework of themes and ideas, and he built on them piece by piece."

On the design side, Blue Q found some wonderful vintage textiles and incorporated old borders, repurposed clip art, and a charming color palette. It was important to create an easy visual rhythm, particularly because the packages are quite text-heavy.

TIP

Nash says, "For a gift manufacturer like Blue Q, a huge majority of its customers are women. Spend time thinking about their fashion sensibility and attitudes. The men can buy neckties!"

THE SHRUNKS

The Shrunks, Canada

PROJECT DESCRIPTION & DESIGN STRATEGY:

The in-house agency for The Shrunks is mostly composed of members of the previous outside agency. This provided a unique set of advantages and disadvantages for ongoing work. The team can manage all forms of marketing and design, creating a consistent message through each layer of customer interaction. But losing a project manager dictated that the creatives manage their own projects.

The brand personality is playful, lively, funky, clean, simple, and cute. Stripes are included in the design as a nostalgic element—harking back to simpler times and cozy pajamas. The brand colors are bright and fun, but they are not typical primary colors commonly found in kids' brands.

Sunny, the loyal guard dog, was developed to help kids fight their fears around bedtime. The child can relate to the face of a puppy and feel protected. The dog sleeps with one eye open just to make sure everything is as it should be. Sunny has an S inside a crest, and it refers to a superhero cape.

TIP

The Shrunks designer, Perry Chua, says, "In designing for the toddler market, one must always remember to design for the parent, who is the ultimate decision maker. The overall look must be cute, friendly, extremely approachable, and just brimming with personality (sayings like 'are we there yet?' on luggage), yet stylish, practical, and well executed. This combination gives both the young consumer and his or her parent the confidence that our products will deliver on our brand promise—making bedtime fun and safe for kids, wherever they are."

Chapter 7
MATERIALS + SUBSTRATES

MATERIAL MATTERS. Full disclosure: Our office has been designed with an obnoxious amount of storage space not because we are neat freaks, but to conceal our design-object hoarding problem. As a group, we have the nasty habit of bringing interesting found objects to the studio with no immediate intent other than to hopefully, someday, leverage their coolness. We suspect other designers have this very same issue. We like wine labels made out of rubber sleeves or even sans label altogether and identified only by a dog-collar-esque leather band and metal charm. These are wonderful examples of unique material decisions that break from convention.

• • •

We appreciate the interesting juxtapositions, the off-purpose use of texture, and the surprising reuse of materials intended for a different audience. It forces consumers to rethink their perceived notion of what a package really is. At the end of the day, a package is designed to invoke our curiosity, inspire us to interact, and ultimately, create a value that is worthy of our hard-earned dollars. We all can admit that sometimes the physical presence of an object in-store is so overwhelming that if we don't purchase it for ourselves, we'll at least consider it for a gift. The power of packaging with interesting materials is a potent motivational tool for creating conversions.

This brings up an interesting point. When deciding to use a nontraditional packaging system, ask yourself, "Is this about utility or awareness?" Often, out-of-the-box material sourcing can run the risk of being so gimmicky that it discourages purchasing in a commoditized market. Fortunately, that same effect is precisely what makes a product so giftable. We talk a lot about giftability at Grip because it is such a powerful tool in the purchasing cycle. When someone gives a gift, they are exposing themselves to judgment. A proper, perhaps even humorous or unexpected package, can go a long way to allaying the fears of the gift giver. Even if the recipient doesn't agree with the product, at least the presentation was fun and interesting. This, of course, is especially salient in the wine market, where individual palates run the gamut, yet an interesting label will go far in explaining the validity of the gift.

Considering the material sourcing differently also forces designers to accept that a more dialed-down approach is best. Several luxury brands have adopted the practice of merely sourcing the heaviest, most luxurious paper, and regardless of the design, this still has a palpable positive effect. Although we cringe every time the typography of a Louis Vuitton bag crosses our monitor, their delivery of product is undeniable with respect to packaging materials from boxes to bags. Tiffany, as well, is well versed in the need for heavy-weight packaging of unprecedented quality. Even though the design is so understated, we can imagine what the box looks and feels like, regardless of the contents.

CARGILL EMPYREAL 75 WINE
Bailey Lauerman, USA

PROJECT DESCRIPTION & DESIGN STRATEGY:

The target audience was pet food manufacturers attending the Pet Food Forum trade show and considering using Cargill's Empyreal 75 protein, a pet food protein supplement for dogs and cats, as an ingredient. For Bailey Lauerman, the solution was to design a limited-edition wine bottle as a gift for the manufacturers that made a strong connection to cats and dogs. "Alley Cat Red" and "Foxhound Red" were selected as the names for the two red wines. Both names adorned the stainless-steel tags that hung from the leather collars.

DEVICE PRINTSHOP
HOLIDAY COFFEE LIQUEUR
Device Creative Collaborative, USA

PROJECT DESCRIPTION & DESIGN STRATEGY:

Device Printshop is a public access letterpress and screenprinting studio located in The Wherehouse, home of Krankies Coffee in Winston-Salem, North Carolina. This coffee liqueur was handmade using Krankies Coffee and moonshine from Piedmont Distillers and given as a holiday gift. The packaging was inspired by the burlap bags used for shipping unroasted beans. The bags were screenprinted using a unique blend of thickened coffee and dye. Hang tags were letterpress printed and stamped.

TIP

Don't let unexpected substrates limit you from exploring them for packaging. Unique concepts will set your project apart from others.

The moral of the story is that materials matter. How someone gauges quality when purchasing items of discretionary value boils down to the packaging. Source something interesting, and a cheap item appears unique and giftable. Source materials reflecting industry-defining quality and the contents can be priced accordingly, regardless of their cost to produce. We, as designers, can implement the strategic direction of how to go to market for our clients with intelligent choices suited to their customers. At the end of the day, our job is to find methods and material sources that create desire among the most likely consumers.

TIP

Studio 32 North was told repeatedly that a real torn edge on the Masterson's paper label could not be produced without paper being torn by hand. However, in further research, they found one diemaker willing to try something new. The goal was to create a unique torn edge on the Masterson's label, which involved using a much more efficient hammer and a rubber mat method. And the outcome was that each label is truly unique. The lesson: it's important to be able to understand when to take "no" for an answer and when to push it.

MASTERSON'S RYE WHISKEY
Studio 32 North, USA

PROJECT DESCRIPTION & DESIGN STRATEGY:

Drawing inspiration from its namesake, the packaging is imbued with Bat Masterson's life and lore. The bottle has a strikingly graceful shoulder that's reminiscent of nineteenth-century whiskey flasks, while the small front label lets the whiskey's glorious amber hue do most of the talking. Serving as a tribute to Masterson's days as a renowned journalist, the die-cut label resembles a clipped-out newspaper column, complete with torn edges like a real newspaper. The exterior box features a die-cut window, allowing the label to stand out, yet fit in seamlessly with newspaper articles printed over the surface of the box. The articles delve deeper into Masterson's life and were custom written in the distinctively verbose and dramatic turn-of-the-century tone.

TREASURE

Supperstudio, Spain

PROJECT DESCRIPTION & DESIGN STRATEGY:

Treasure is a unique winery in a submarine in the Bay of Biscay. After maturing in oak barrels the wine is placed under the sea, where it's continuously controlled by biologists and wine makers. This is where it acquires its surprising character, at the same time creating an artificial reef where more than eighty different species of marine life have been identified. Supperstudio crafted the branded packaging focused on two pillars: the flavor and the authentic personality of a wine rocked in the ocean and the recovery project of the sea flora and fauna.

They designed an iconic look for the bottle, which is stamped directly onto the glass, a simple one-color silkscreen. This practically naked bottle is delivered to the consumer in very special packaging: three perforated pieces and one solid piece of corrugated cardboard make up the package in which the bottle is housed. Two rubber bands hold the packaging together and protect the treasure within.

TIP

Simple, recycled, and out-of-context materials for this product make it feel like something else entirely—befitting its name, Treasure. Not only is this solution unique and gift-worthy, it's also economically sound and environmentally friendly. You can't ask much more of packaging.

UNCLE VAL'S BOTANICAL GIN
Studio 32 North, USA

PROJECT DESCRIPTION & DESIGN STRATEGY:

Inspired by bitter bottles from the eighteenth and nineteenth centuries, Uncle Val's bottle was manufactured in Italy and possesses strong, tapered shoulders and a dark green, antique hue. The label is also reminiscent of old-world spirit labels, featuring an ornate cursive font, a tastefully understated color palette, and a Roman coin–styled illustration of Uncle Val. Each bottle has one of three bottom labels featuring some of Uncle Val's more notable sayings. Together, the bottle, labels, and gin itself evoke a dedication to craftsmanship that is still very much alive in the old world of Uncle Val's Italy.

TIP

Along with the beauty of the bottle came the challenge of its tapered shape. Designer Sallie Reynolds Allen says, "Getting the two different labels to line up as they crossed three sides of the bottle was a bit trying and required some geometrical thinking. It helped to use the artwork as guides to delineate folds."

54-40
Bureau of Betterment, USA

||||||||||||||||||||||||||||||||||||||||||||||||||||||||||||||||||||||||||||||||||||

PROJECT DESCRIPTION & DESIGN STRATEGY:

The 54-40 packaging project was a collaboration between the packaging designer and product designer. The packaging structure is inspired by the jig used to assemble each state. A piece of charcoal-colored chipboard is sandwiched between layers of thick cardboard that mimic the topographic nature of the product and show off the rich wood color. The front of the packaging is laser cut with the pattern of surrounding states while product information is shown on the back panel. The product is easily nestled into its own shape with a small finger hole on the back to help pop it out for use. The packaging doubles as a freestanding display for the state.

TIP

Testing the packaging materials early uncovered the laser-cutting depth, tolerance for lasering typography, and durability. Working together with the product design team from the start was crucial to finding a fully realized and integrated solution.

MAGNETIC
FREE-STANDING DISPL
LASER CUT & HAND ASSEMBLED
IN PORTLAND, OREGON

54 40
FIFTYFOURFORTY.COM

HOLD AND HOLLO
Örsi Juhász, Hungary

||||||||||||||||||||||||||||||||||||||||||||||||||||||||||||||||||||||||||||

PROJECT DESCRIPTION & DESIGN STRATEGY:

Paper labels are widely used as the default material for wine bottles. They provide room to display typical information and assist in creating the mood of the product. Örsi Juhász created a label made from silicone for Hold and Hollo. This unique substrate does more than house typography, color, and information. The tactile quality and color make it irresistible for potential buyers to pick up and hold the product. Furthermore, silicone labels are easy to print, and in this case can be removed, returned, or reused.

TIP

Materials and manufacturing are typically more affordable options in China. Problems that arise can be challenging to solve, such as the deformed text with Hold and Hollo. The expert vendor was able to solve the silicone production issues, but the manufacturing process was extremely slow due to the distance between the design firm and the manufacturing facility.

ALTERNATIVE ORGANIC

The Creative Method, Australia

PROJECT DESCRIPTION & DESIGN STRATEGY:

The brief was to name and create a premium organic package for a limited-edition organic Marlborough sauvignon blanc wine. It needed to look and feel natural as well as act as a talking point for consumers. Alternative was chosen, as it reflects a new way of looking at organic packaging. The concept simply showed a vine: from the leaves to the bark to the wine. Every aspect of the packaging was organic, including the laser-cut balsa wood, the string and wax that is used to affix the label to the bottle, the outer paper wrapping, and even the inks used to print the image.

TIP

Look into vendor possibilities before designing a package. Laser cutting and etching can achieve fine details that die-cutting cannot. Your vendor can show you what is possible or inspire you to push boundaries. Bring them on as a partner early on for the most efficient relationship.

PORTLAND MUSEUM OF ART
Might & Main, USA

PROJECT DESCRIPTION & DESIGN STRATEGY:

Might & Main designed the identity, packaging, and product line for an exhibit at the Portland Museum of Art. Named as one of the top museum shows of 2012 by Fodor's, the exhibit was a comprehensive retrospective on the life and work of Winslow Homer.

Homer's life was complex and rich; he was equally at home in high society, hunting and fishing in the wild, or painting alone on a bluff overlooking the ocean. Those diverse influences informed everything about the line created for the museum, from materials and production methods to color. The touch of red that carries through the line was inspired by Homer's own regular use of a splash of vermilion and a rusty-colored signature.

Might & Main began with an identity system, creating a family of logo marks to define two distinct families of products: the unexpected and highly customized Homer-inspired lifestyle items, and the more traditional museum store items, such as totes and mugs. To round out the project, they designed a cohesive labeling and packaging system that positions the entire range of products and packaging within the same family. It also provides backstory on Homer and the production partners. Aside from the higher-end luxury items, a whimsical bobblehead and accompanying package design were added to the lineup with broad appeal for the young, old, and nonchalant visitor.

Source vendors locally for unique and custom printing or manufacturing. Might & Main sought out local artists and craftspeople to create limited-edition items that were both contemporary and reminiscent of Homer's life and times. These items included a line of zippered map cases and linen pillows (constructed by Black Point Mercantile) from repurposed painters' drop cloths, a line of broadsides featuring Homerian quotes (printed with vintage wooden type on an antique press by Strong Arm Bindery), handmade soaps in scents evocative of the Maine coast (by Casco Bay Soap Co.), and dandy handkerchiefs sewn by hand (by Molly Angie).

now FRESH®

under 12 mo
kitten

made with
100% fresh
turkey, salmon,
duck & omega oils

0%

grain free
rendered meats
by-products
gluten, wheat, corn or soy
artificial preservatives

Balanced proteins & fats for growth
DHA & EPA to support brain development
Pre & probiotics for sensitive stomachs

Feline Diet | Régime pour chat
Net Wt. 4 lb (1.81kg)

Chapter 8

BRAND REFRESH

COMMAND-R, COMMAND CASH. When the economic implosion sapped all of the R&D money out of most companies, we noticed a peculiar trend: repackaging and refreshing of legacy brands. Over time we came to understand that, in lieu of spending large sums to launch products, companies were retooling their packages to promote what was currently moving product in a down economy.

• • •

S ome companies even took advantage of reduced competition to secure more shelf space and worked their packaging systems to accommodate merchandising in multiples. Other firms moved to address value propositions by noting (or inflating) the sense of scale with packaged consumables. At the very least, this trend recognized that changing the single most important conversion mechanism, the package, would be a worthwhile investment. This goes double for those companies relying on fewer products for the majority of their sales. This comes from the Pareto Principle, a common rule of thumb in business where 80 percent of effects come from 20 percent of the causes—in this case 80 percent of the revenue comes from 20 percent of the products.

Just as ties and pant legs go from skinny to wide, so too, packaging needs to maintain a sense of timeliness to retain consumer confidence. While retro packaging has its occasional appeal, it is best kept occasional. Shoppers today are influenced by an unprecedented amount of information hurled at them through many different outlets. To stand out from the crowd, consider consistency among brand offerings of the same category. A consumer whipping through the beer aisle, inundated with countless craft beer brands, is more likely to notice a company if there is some consistency of tone, color, illustration, and typography. Perhaps that alone will be cause for pause, versus the almost certain flyover of the overwrought, overdescribed, text-heavy design that seems to plague most craft beers. Without sounding curt, we promise not to make a brewer drink our bathtub beer if they promise not to make us use their bad-pun beer name and 2,500-word description of what went into the bottle. It's a good deal for everyone.

SANDBAR

Grip, USA

PROJECT DESCRIPTION & DESIGN STRATEGY:

The initial version of this package did not accurately convey the quality and craftsmanship of the spirit. This is fairly common: When a new spirit comes to market, it's typically on the cheapest route possible. Then, as the product finds its fan base and gains a bit of ground in the marketplace, it often hits a plateau and is limited in growth due to any number of factors, one being an outdated package that doesn't have broad appeal or may not be sophisticated enough to compete against other products in the same category. This was the case for Sandbar Rum. The client asked for a reference to pirates (see tip below) and the Outer Banks, since location is such a critical part of the story of the rum. The redesign utilized a very simple, and very economical, black and white solution. The bottle is fully spray-coated with black ink first, then screenprinted 360 degrees with opaque white. It's an uncommon aesthetic for rum (and other "vacation-drink" spirits), which gives it distinction and memorability.

TIP

Just because a client asks for a cliché doesn't mean you have to deliver one. This bottle was inspired by a pirate theme without using all of the old visual standards. It draws on some of the more intriguing (nostalgic script type) and mysterious (sailing in the pitch dark), rather than the themed elements that have been overused and obvious.

89

O n occasion we encounter projects—and trust us when we say you will too—where a brand has managed to get to market with an inexpensive, homemade package only to find their sales stall at a certain point in their growth. Typically, they come to us for advice on marketing that ends with advice on packaging. The package is the *ultimate* point of sale, and if there is a disconnect between the story being told and the product promise or consumer expectation, sales are sacrificed. We once had clients from a rum company convinced that a strong pirate theme and like-spirited copy was the essence of their brand. The problem was that the likely consumer for that type of product was a cost-conscious buyer, and their product was not exactly, uh, cost-conscious. In fact, the rum was high quality, and at its core the brand story should allow the wealthy vacationers of the Outer Banks to bring a little vacation memory back home. Our challenge was to design an elegant package that would convey the quality of the product to consumers, while also playing up the spirit of irreverence that pirate culture is known for. Other design issues involved playing down the pirate-speak while making sure to connect with Johnny Depp's Captain Jack, NOT Somali pirate connotations.

Our solution involved spraying the bottle a matte black (very pirate-y) with an elegant woodcut illustration (very old-world). Type was tastefully arranged while focusing the copy on the "Spirit of the Outer Banks" (very luxury-brand). Full disclosure: To win the larger battle, we did have to accommodate a small "Yo-Ho-Ho" on one of the illustrations. At the end of the day, you win rum, you lose some.

ARCADIA ALES
Grip, USA

PROJECT DESCRIPTION & DESIGN STRATEGY:

Arcadia beers are produced in small batches at the Battle Creek brewery using methods originated in England, and each style of beer reflects over 250 years of world-class brewing heritage. As new brews were created and added to their ever-growing line of bottled products, the style and design of each label grew more disparate and varied, and the overall Arcadia family of beers had no visual congruence or consistent branding. The old labels also did not reflect the level of craftsmanship in each artisanal brew. The rebrand looks at each beer like a work of art, and the labels themselves have been transformed into tiny, stunning artworks, tying the name of each brew to the story behind it with a custom illustration in the style of old travel posters and flyers from the early twentieth century. The client (and their customers) loved the illustrations so much that they made them into posters as well—full circle with that inspiration!

NOW FRESH
Subplot Design, Canada

PROJECT DESCRIPTION & DESIGN STRATEGY:

Petcurean Pet Nutrition was founded in 1999 as a small start-up company, based on a unique concept that utilizes concentrated forms of meat and human-grade ingredients to formulate a pet food that replicates what families enjoy at home every day. When examining the almost 100 SKUs of packaging in Petcurean's most popular lines, it was critical to expand beyond the corporate identity to connect the unique propositions and benefits of the products themselves with the consumers who purchase them. Before the rebrand, Petcurean Pet Nutrition's product lines were similar in design and substrate, and offered little distinction for the consumer.

The concept that "it could only be fresher if you made it from scratch" truly sets this product apart from other product lines, and the packaging expresses this through "Fresh Market" signage, burlap textures, and familiar produce labels. Soft, warm, natural, and intrinsically connected to the notion of market freshness, the package informs the reader about the superior fresh ingredients and specific life-stage recipes.

GOOD BOY

BAKED ORGANIC

BOP

SEA SALT

65% LESS FAT
THAN REGULAR
POTATO CHIPS‡

CERTIFIED
GF
GLUTEN-FREE
™

FLAVORED POTATO CRISPS

ORGANIC!

www.BOPSnacks.com

USDA
ORGANIC

ORGANIC
OVEN
BAKED
FOR GREAT TAST

Chapter 9
COLOR

COLOR COMMENTARY. While common legend has it that a pot of gold lies at the end of the rainbow, for package designers, the real gold is contained within the rainbow, and how well a product can evoke emotion through color. In many instances, we can name a product category, and the color associated with it is so obvious that choosing outside of the cliché is revelatory.

•••

W hat color package would a new eco-friendly, organic plant fertilizer come in? We are willing to bet no one guessed anything other than some version of green. Accepting that color is emotional and is so often tied to a specific set of preconceived notions, it is a powerful tool to create separation in the marketplace.

When the popular light-bondage and sex toy company Sex and Mischief noted the popularity of the *Fifty Shades of Grey* book series, they immediately retooled their packages to reflect the book jacket design. With monochromatic gray-scale imagery and dramatic lighting their packages are easy to spot. When viewed in context of a wall of vibrantly hued— how should we phrase this?—other such products, the Sex and Mischief items look decidedly upscale. By co-opting an existing brand's recognition and popularity, consumer comfort is also enhanced, and some of the anxiety the category inherently creates upon purchase is relieved. Color, or in this case the lack thereof, will always have to live in an environment, and as a designer, your active decision to differentiate from the norm is powerful.

Differentiation is important, but on the flip side of the color wheel (apologies, we couldn't resist), when you have a product whose benefits are as dubious as the salty snack category, tapping into the emotion of a color can be your best tool. Baked chip manufacturer BOPS utilized what can best be described as an "uplifting" color palette for their line of chips and in doing so, creates an uplifting sense of cheer. Note too that there are thousands of shades (yes, more than fifty) of any particular color, and tapping the emotion of a hue is the key to standing out on a shelf and with consumers. In the BOPS instance, they didn't use just any red, blue, green, or orange, they used versions of each color that had pep and vibrancy. Purchasing snack chips is typically not a remorseful occurrence, and the proper color system, combined with the right product, can activate our subconscious decision-making process. Perhaps the market is ready for an all-black, tear-streaked box of chocolate-covered peanut and potato-chip clusters specifically for post-breakup bingeing. We can see the ad now: BOPS is proud to announce our Big Box of F*ck-It—snacks to fill the gaping hole in your heart. Might work.

BOPS
A3 Design, USA

|||||||||||||||||||||||||||||||||||||||||||||||||||||||||||||||

PROJECT DESCRIPTION & DESIGN STRATEGY:

Sales of the typical potato chip skyrocket during the summer months. With design elements that pay homage to the idea of the family picnic, the BOPS chip packaging cleverly evokes nostalgia while calling out the nutritional value of the product. The goal was to create a package without any of the typical visual clichés of organic snacks, such as earthy-neutral colors, in order to compete with the big guys and their greasy chips. The product had to stand out as nutritionally superior and still invoke the notion that this product would satisfy a consumer's craving for a salty, crunchy snack.

TIP

Always get a printed proof—as color accurate as possible—before the full production run. Inks respond differently to every packaging surface, and some color finessing may be needed to get the true color intended. A shiny chip bag holds color differently than a matte cereal box, so even if you've printed a particular color before, a new substrate may introduce different challenges and should be thoroughly tested.

COLORFUL CHARACTERS.

Imagine a Tiffany's box, a can of Coca-Cola, or McDonald's Golden Arches. Chances are a specific color would come to mind. Consistent use of color in packaging can create a tremendous shortcut to the brand values and aesthetic of a company. It is for this exact reason that we advise against repurposing a blue box from Tiffany for a gift of, say, free drink cards from Starbucks. Trust us.

The moral of the story is that color can become a character that represents the brand all by itself. True, this is not an easy process and demands very strict policing, and the product must be merchandised and promoted to near saturation, but the fact remains that color resonates fast and deep with consumers. When considering a package design, ask yourself this: If colors all communicate something emotional (e.g., green is healthy, yellow is exciting, etc.), what one color would best inform your most likely consumer that this product is targeted to them? Is there an analogous color in the company color way? If so, tailor your design around the existing brand equity and paint that box boldly!

That noted, one of the biggest mistakes we see in package design is an overuse of color for emphasis. Just like the hierarchy for type, color too must be dealt with using an obvious order and prioritization. When everything screams, nothing is heard. Some of our favorite examples of excellent use of color ways involve broad swaths of a single midtone that can then be knocked out of or overprinted on. This essentially empowers a single hue to communicate on several levels and gives whatever "pop" color you choose room to breathe and, well, pop!

ELKARITA

idgroup, USA

PROJECT DESCRIPTION & DESIGN STRATEGY:

Elkarita was recently introduced to the marketplace as a 100% natural, no-sugar-added, nonalcoholic cocktail mixer that is perfect for diabetics and the health conscious. While that positioning normally conjures up images of serious and straightforward package visuals, these bottles are anything but. The bright and playful color palette immediately establishes a fun and cheerful brand. The health-conscious mixers remind us that it's possible to have our cake...er, low-calorie cocktail...and drink it too.

MODERN TIMES BEER
Helms Workshop, USA

||||||||||||||||||||||||||||||||||||||||||||||||||||||||||||||||||||||

PROJECT DESCRIPTION & DESIGN STRATEGY:

Modern Times founder Jacob McKean has a unique vision for his brewery, and it proved to be a perfect fit for design firm Helms Workshop. Christian Helms states, "We do our best work with clients who aren't afraid to have a point of view, and who are brave enough to stand apart as different in a crowded marketplace. Modern Times has that in spades."

The brewery was named after a utopian community founded in New York in 1850, and the brand narrative was modeled after historic visionaries and their dreams of the future. Helms Workshop therefore explored a host of design directions referencing forward-thinking historic icons including Raymond Loewy and Norman Bel Geddes, as well as contemporary revisionists like Wes Anderson.

TIP

Look for clients who were inspired by someone or something truly unique and interesting, and you'll have plenty of research fodder and exploratory roads to follow. It's much easier, and ultimately more genuine and poignant, to craft a visual brand when the original product story is compelling and unique. The client was so thrilled with the final Modern Times packaging, he says, "The cans are so devastatingly tasteful, a koozie would be a crime."

TIP

Explore options for potential line extensions. Midnight Moonshine will eventually include a fruit-infused line, and the original black-and-white design is the perfect canvas for adding ingredient-inspired pops of color to build out the product line.

MIDNIGHT MOONSHINE
Device Creative Collaborative, USA

PROJECT DESCRIPTION & DESIGN STRATEGY:

Few family recipes carry a jail sentence, but for the Johnson family it was a way of life; with the law on his heels, Junior ran the finest moonshine to the dry rural south. This product story is captured beautifully on the labels for the current refined moonshine, a triple-distilled, lower-proof, and more legal version of the original. Drawing inspiration from the design of Johnson's cars, used for running moonshine in the 1930s and 1940s, the packaging is simple, bold, and stunning in black and white. The restrained color palette perfectly evokes the Prohibition era and stands out on the shelf among much busier, color-heavy packages.

GO!
Subplot Design Inc., USA

PROJECT DESCRIPTION & DESIGN STRATEGY:

"Created to put more life into your pet"
trumpets the GO! product positioning,
and the packaging brings this to life with
black-and-white action shots of real pets,
complete with heartwarming testimonials
of health and revitalization. The package
itself brings an "active lifestyle" sensibility
to the pet specialty store shelf with the
black-and-white portraits, color coding for
formula identification, and callouts for recipe
ingredients and benefits.

TIP

*Always visualize and plan for how a
family of products will be merchandised
and perused by potential customers. Side
by side, these packages create a very strong
"shelf billboard," and the clever use of color
gives the brand a strong overall palette
while individually identifying each recipe
in the product line and drawing attention
to the critical benefits for consumers'
four-legged friends.*

JOE'S ICE CREAM
Unreal, UK

|||||||||||||||||||||||||||||||||||||||||||||||||||||||||||||||||||||||||||||||||||||||

PROJECT DESCRIPTION & DESIGN STRATEGY:

Joe's Ice Cream is a local ice cream made in Wales since 1922 and has a huge national and international following. Customers and fans travel from near and far just to get their fix of the popular and tasty treats, often saying it's the "best ice cream in the world." The new branding and packaging pays homage to the brand's cult following by featuring descriptive brand and flavor phrases in a nostalgic typographic style. Support for the redesign has poured in from online social media.

TIP

There are certain expected rules when it comes to color and flavor perception. For example, chocolate ice cream packaging would naturally be brown. But when unique flavors prompt unsavory color combinations, the designer must find a balance between effective color representation and aesthetics.

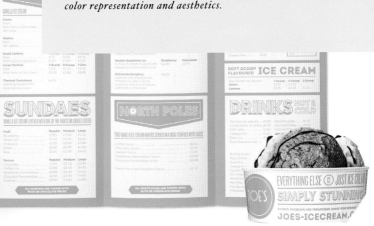

Vosges

love goddess
CHOCOLATE CAKE MIX

{ Made with premium cacao
& French sea salt }

NET WT 23.9 OZ (679 g)

Vosges

mo's bacon
CHOCOLATE CHIP
PANCAKE MIX

(4 oz. of
Mo's Bacon Bar
inside!)

NET WT 16 OZ (454 g)

Chapter 10
PHOTOGRAPHY + STYLING

PICTURE, PERFECT. We all know that blister packs (those clear, difficult-to-open plastic packages) sell product because they show product. That we would rather open a blister than a blister-packaged product tells you how we feel about them. The one opportunity that clear or see-through packaging misses is the opportunity to actively shape the way a product appears.

• • •

As Martha Stewart and Barbara Walters can attest, the right lens, with the right styling, makes all the difference. Fuzzy, soft focus aside, we relish the opportunity to be involved in product shoots for packaging purposes. Exaggerating scale on a package is one of our favorite techniques that allows fly-by shoppers to quickly understand the quality of small product details. Likewise, attention to very small details in wide-angle shots allows the opportunity to subtly show a product's intended use. We could write several books on how food photography is styled, lit, and shot, but let's just say it is a complex art that is critical to product sales and always dominates consumable-packaging design.

While Photoshop is ubiquitous, and occasionally we wonder if anything is real, our firm belief is to get it right on camera, and everything you do after will be that much easier. Beyond a photography tutorial, it is important to arm yourself with the tools of a stylist, regardless of the type of shoot. Small brushes, wipes of all variety, cans of air, and matting lotion are all handy tools. Several resources are available online to help you equip yourself, but the most successful photography and styling is less about technique and more about concept and understanding the end use. Quick comps with stock images are one way we create immediate storyboards to evaluate a photo's potential on the package. Beginning with a quick "sketch" like this will liberate you to consider all of the small but crucial details when it comes to the real shoot.

Never forget that photography gives you the opportunity to exaggerate reality. We are not suggesting this be done in any nefarious manner, but instead to cut to the emotion of the product. How can a product have emotion? Simply put, anything we choose in life, we create some emotional bond. The items that we interact with the most are part of our purchasing habit-loop. On some level, these products just "work" for us. Some purchases help to define our style, some items provide utility, and some can even make us laugh. Next time you are out shopping, look into your cart and note how your purchases make you feel. Then examine the package and see if that emotion is played to through photography. This is the key to converting consumers from browser to buyer. Use this power wisely.

VOSGES CHEESE & CHOCOLATE
Wink Design Atelier, USA

PROJECT DESCRIPTION & DESIGN STRATEGY:

A sensory experience for foodies and cheese and chocolate addicts, this collection from Vosges comes in an etched bamboo box and includes a curated variety of cheeses and chocolates to pair, taste, and experience. It also includes a forty-page guidebook and cheese markers to identify the cheeses for your guests. The box was created as a keepsake, handcrafted in Indonesia, with a cheese board as the lid. The photographs of the collection allow a consumer to visualize the spread on her very own table, invoking the sensory experience of tasting these savory morsels.

TIP

As any chef will tell you, the hardest part of a complicated meal is timing. Complex packaging projects are no different—coordinating each element to be completed, delivered, and collated with the rest of the components can be the greatest challenge. Planning and organization are your greatest assets.

B y now we are certain that most of you have enjoyed a little *schadenfreude*-tinged entertainment in the form of Photoshop horrors blog posts. Beyond missing limbs on models and impossible proportions, our advice on retouching is simple: Minimize it. Everyone recognizes that we live in a hyperreal world, but precisely because *nothing* can be trusted, truth in advertising has a tendency to work. At Grip, we are huge advocates of transparency, and while this doesn't mean we refuse to retouch, it does mean that in our styling, we tend to let the product speak for itself. Full disclosure: our company headshots feature ridiculously white teeth and perhaps a freckle or two less than what you'll get if you see us in person.

VOSGES HAUT–CHOCOLAT BAKING MIXES

Wink Design Atelier, USA

PROJECT DESCRIPTION & DESIGN STRATEGY:

The Vosges Haut–Chocolat line of baking mixes allows their customers to create a bit of Vosges in their own kitchen. While most of the Vosges products feature imagery focused on the exotic ingredients, the baking line took the opposite approach and portrays the finished product on the outside of each box. The silhouetted images of each item are striking in their simplicity and beautifully tie the line of baking mixes together as a family.

When planning, styling, or art directing a photo shoot for product packaging, carefully consider the impact of props. Each product in the baking mixes line uses a different utensil, giving a bit more personality to the product inside. Together, the utensils unify the product line, even though they are used quite subtly within the photography. A creative twist was employed for the sugar cookie mix: The "utensil" is a child's hand, supporting the copy "Great for Kids!".

Chapter 11

DESIGNING FOR FOOD

PAVLOV'S PACKAGE. The grocery list is checked off, and on the way to the register something catches your eye. There it is, oozing caramel with giant peanuts and chocolate whose melty perfection appears to have been made from the hand of God. So you grab and go. Whether you are buying this candy bar as a habit of treating yourself to a brand you love, or are impulse buying because the promise of something delicious was too much to refuse, the package was the ultimate point of sale for that product.

• • •

Food is a funny category and truthfully, deserves an entire book dedicated to the singular subject alone. (Are you listening, Rockport? Ahem.) Seriously, packaging for consumables has a myriad of unique considerations, including food safety, allowable inks and waxes, and nutritional information. Oh, and the beloved FDA. That noted, our advice for when a consumable package project crosses your desk for the first time is to employ the single greatest tool any designer has...the phone. Yes, the phone. Call friends and find vendors who work with foodstuffs. They will know "the rules" when it comes to package requirements and often have contacts, or even people on staff, that check for FDA regulations and the like. Set up calls, and when you find someone you like, make an appointment to meet in person and go armed with a list of questions. Show them your ideas and get them on board at the earliest possible juncture and, if appropriate, hoist the technical requirements onto their shoulders. A word of warning: We rarely experience problems with the work we are able to contain within the walls of Grip from start to finish. Trouble happens when we let outside vendors manage the project. Our advice is to stay extremely vigilant with project time frames, scope,

and double-checking governmental and food safety requirements. We said you could off-load the technical aspects of production, not the responsibility for the outcome.

All that noted, here is what is great: Food packaging is fun. We typically get a lot of samples, pack on a few pounds, and spend time doing ethnographic research into the specific market. We wholeheartedly encourage anyone designing for food to spend time in the environment where the product will ultimately be merchandised. Many of these areas will be in pay-to-play shelf space, and if you do not accommodate for that, your design may get lost in the cluttered environment. If your package stands out, the product will sell out and you'll have a client for life.

Window die-cuts and enhanced food photography are naturals in this category because monkey-see, monkey-buy. Maybe that's why bananas don't come in boxes. If we look beyond the obvious nature of showing the product, a few other trends start to show themselves. We noticed that several categories were so stagnant that it almost seemed like fear of change outweighed the necessity to stand out on a shelf. A good example of this is flour, which seems like it would not need much design—the product was a commoditized

GUZMAN Y GOMEZ
MEXICAN TAQUERIA
The Creative Method, Australia

PROJECT DESCRIPTION & DESIGN STRATEGY:

While Mexican food and vibrant Latin culture are strongly represented all over the world, they were not very visible in pre-2006 Australia. Taco Bell had come into Australia and failed. The Creative Method knew nothing about Mexican food or designing for restaurant chains. They researched other fast-food restaurants and how they were wired. They immersed themselves in Mexican culture and admitted they slept very little for the three months during the project's creation.

The packaging captures the brand look and dials up the personality and attitude. GYG salsas feature store employees' reactions to the salsas and express the strength and potency of each sauce. Captions printed on the bottles link the staff's personal history to the authentic Mexican products. The cups, bags, taco boxes, and burrito wraps stand out with the bold yellow, black, and white images from Mexico.

TIP

Understand the market for whom you are working. Understand the rules and motivations of the client's client. Immerse yourself in a foreign culture if you don't understand it. Then have fun bringing the product to life.

necessity purchased by bakers who tended to stick with legacy brands. Then along came Tesco, who literally and figuratively dusted the competition. Take a look for yourself and tell us that when given a choice, you wouldn't pick this over the same old, same old. Since then, several companies have rethought their flour packaging and come out with more innovative, modern versions of the once-ubiquitous flour bag. That's the power of the package.

ONE FINAL NOTE: Opportunities to design for wide-release foodstuffs are rare, because those jobs tend to go to agencies with a specialized focus. If you really want an entry into the market, consider working with a restaurant to develop its carryout packaging. Often overlooked and ordered from the usual large suppliers, carryout packaging is a wonderful opportunity to advertise a restaurant in the one place it matters most: an existing diner's fridge! Or consider how impactful someone walking down the street with branded carryout packaging is. Essentially, a customer becomes a walking billboard and most likely spreads the brand to other, likely consumers. This alone is too powerful to miss, and we encourage our

hospitality clients to develop branded containers, not because it is cool, but because it works better than an ad in some paper read by people unlikely to ever set foot inside the establishment. Compare that to the likelihood that anyone who has leftovers in the fridge will have a social circle likely to want similar products, and you have a can't-miss promotional opportunity.

STOP THE WORLD CAFE
Fusion Design Company, UK

PROJECT DESCRIPTION & DESIGN STRATEGY:

The threefold challenge was to design and develop a cake box that 1) could be stored flat; 2) could hold six cupcakes or cake slices; and 3) could be made from a single sheet using no glue. Additionally, the design had to be eye-catching and serve as a mini-billboard promoting the café during transport within the United Kingdom.

TIP

Test the die line in real-world scenarios. Fusion Design Company ensured different cupcakes and cake slices would fit without cream touching the box or allowing the product to move once packaged and carried home.

ÈLIA AROMATIC OLIVE OILS

Atipus, Spain

PROJECT DESCRIPTION & DESIGN STRATEGY:

Èlia is a feminine name derived from the Greek word for "olive." In accordance with its name, a subtle feminine touch has been given to both the brand and the packaging itself. Èlia's first product is a selection of aromatic oils.

HOORAY PURÉE

Grip, USA

PROJECT DESCRIPTION & DESIGN STRATEGY:

Invested in finding realistic ways to help people eat more vegetables, Hooray Purée is a convenient and effective way to add valuable nutrients to any diet. A bright color palette combined with sophisticated details attracts adults and children alike.

Hooray Purée was initially sold in the freezer aisle at Costco, a big-box store. To appeal to that target market, the product was sold in a variety pack. Feedback from customers and experts on staff had two major concerns. The first: The product packs looked like Popsicles (and were stocked not far away from actual Popsicles), and confused the customer as

to how it should be consumed. Second: *freshness*, *healthy*, and *pure* are not typically equated with a frozen product. To solve that product issue, the current version of the product was developed as a shelf-stable product.

The packaging uses die-cuts to show the fresh pack inside so buyers can see the actual purée. Illustration and photography are used to explain the product quickly, inspire usage, and show convenience. Best of all, the visuals show how delicious and fun nutritious food should be.

With new-to-market products, smaller production runs and budgets don't always allow for grandiose, über-custom packaging solutions. Design big and source smart, and you'll be able to retool existing packaging product components, like these tins, already available in the market for a final product that looks custom. As a product experiences success, higher production runs and budgets will yield the opportunity to take an interim solution to the next level of customization. We're hoping one day our original vision of having these tins hand-pounded out of copper and labels individually painted on by elves will come to fruition. A goat can dream?

THE FLAVOR
BY STEPHANIE IZARD
Grip, USA

PROJECT DESCRIPTION & DESIGN STRATEGY:

Stephanie Izard is the Bravo's season four Top Chef winner and owns two highly successful restaurants in Chicago. She asked Grip to design, position, and name a line of sauces and rubs that would be sold in grocery stores nationwide and at her restaurants. The flavors are derived from popular dishes at her restaurants, Girl & the Goat and Little Goat Diner. The product messaging encourages experienced chefs and casual cooks to experiment with typical recipes and quickly transform them into restaurant-quality meals. The tone is clever and conversational. The initial project scope included just three sauces and one rub. The naming system allowed for any number of rubs or sauces to be added after the initial launch. The messaging illustrates a wide range of potential uses and doesn't limit the product to a particular vegetable or meat dish. Customized type treatments reflect the character and flavor of each product, allowing each product to have its own personality while still maintaining a consistent aesthetic across the line. Being merchandised in both grocery stores and within the restaurant, the design had to evoke the essence of the restaurant experience, while still being shelf-ready for mass distribution.

TIP

The tins elevate the product from a simple spice bag into a thoughtful gift item and keepsake. We've overheard people talking about how they intend to use the tins once the spices are gone— everything from storing jewelry to housing other herbs. Whatever the case (pun intended), it's always a good thing when consumers hang on to the packaging long after the original purpose.

VOSGES HAUT-CHOCOLAT RED FIRE COLLECTION

Wink Design Atelier, USA

PROJECT DESCRIPTION & DESIGN STRATEGY:

Vosges Haut-Chocolat's goal is to help customers travel the world through chocolate. The Red Fire Collection from Vosges Haut-Chocolat contains chocolate-covered tortilla chips, pecans, and sweet toffee infused with chiles and cinnamon. Tubes wrapped with photography separate the collection from the high-end luxury truffles.

TIP

Products should be distinguishable within a brand lineup. The Red Fire Collection confuses customers despite different product names and container sizes, because they all use the same image of the mariachi band.

Designer Brenda Rotheiser Bergen says, "If I were to design this collection again, I would use different images for each product. Using the same image resulted in customers thinking it is the same product, just a different-size container. I learned that the name alone is not enough to differentiate the products from each other."

TIP

Keep pushing an idea. The design criteria for Over the Moon Dairy were to make it feel like a boutique product. The Creative Method started out with a simple hand-drawn logo, but it didn't feel quite right. The identity became much stronger with the addition of a looping tail beneath the logo type in the shape of a moon.

OVER THE MOON DAIRY CO.
The Creative Method, Australia

PROJECT DESCRIPTION & DESIGN STRATEGY:

Over the Moon Dairy Co. asked The Creative Method to name and develop an identity for a boutique New Zealand cheese company. It needed to stand out in local delicatessens amongst the many traditional European brands. And it needed to have a friendly, contemporary, and handcrafted feel.

Personality, craft, and a contemporary edge are reflected in the rough, hand-penciled type for the nursery rhyme Hey Diddle Diddle. It has personality and attitude and is a visual fork in the road from the historical approaches of the competition. This gives a motherly warmth to the packaging and reinforces the handcrafted nature of the cheese-making process.

Chapter 12

HUMOR

FUNNY OR BUY. Is there anyone out there who doesn't like humor? We live for it. Conveying that in a package design, however, is incredibly difficult. Often, humor is topical, or ironic, but both of those forms often fail miserably when applied to something as context-free and necessarily timeless as package design.

• • •

How can a designer incorporate a sense of fun into package design? Let go of trying to be outright funny and agree to be clever, silly, or perhaps even whimsical. "Not Your Grandma's Riesling" is a great example of whimsy. Granted, wine labels are a pretty easy category to incorporate a little comedy into, but understanding the misconception that the wine itself had to overcome, and then turning the name into a parody of the stereotype, is both clever in tone and effective at generating interest.

Other products that benefit from humor are those that are often uncomfortable to purchase. While we fully admit our slightly deviant nature, the act of purchasing lubricant or sex toys still makes us blush a bit. Enter, comedy. One of the most clever package designs we have seen in the sex industry is for two-person lubricant. Fitting together in a manner consistent with the, er, intended usage is both a physical wink-wink and a practical design solution. We can only imagine the hilarity that ensued during comping the design.

Much like Gilbert Gottfried, Sarah Silverman, or Dane Cook, sometimes the fastest way to a chuckle is to let loose and get in your buyer's face. Soaps like You Smell and Dirty Girl are not shy about the way they speak to their consumer. Irreverence toward category norms is usually good for a laugh, and we encourage everyone to try pitching one concept that utilizes this formula, unless it will offend a client.

The holy grail (coveted rubber chicken, perhaps) in our office is to inject a design with something clever. We love when a package can surprise us with something that may be missed at first blush. Consider that most of us interact with the same products over and over, so the joy of discovering something new and fun is revelatory. This same concept is why so many software developers hide "cookies" into popular apps. It only takes a second to add a funny line to the inside flap of a box or write "ouch, that hurt" on the inside of a zip-strip enclosure. Finding the humor in the strangest locations is sure to bring a smile to anyone's face, and if you are able to achieve that, rest assured the world is a happier place.

NOT YOUR GRANDMA'S RIESLING

TypeSpace, Australia

PROJECT DESCRIPTION & DESIGN STRATEGY:

The goal for this wine is to show off the best of Australia's Eden Valley Riesling to both fanatical Riesling lovers and to the Riesling uninitiated. Using a bold name, humor, and contemporary type put old preconceptions about the wine to rest, so this bottle can confidently shine in its modern glory.

TIP

Keeping costs down and creating a striking package design do not have to be mutually exclusive. This label employs only two colors but deftly uses bright ink on a simple white label for a powerful result.

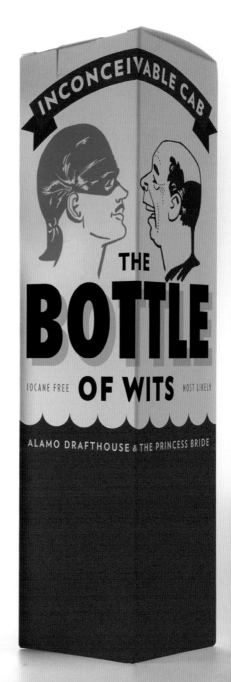

THE BOTTLE OF WITS
Helms Workshop, USA

IIIIIIIIIIIIIIIIIIIIIIIIIIIIIIIIIIIIIIIIIIIIIIIIIIIIIIIIIIIIIIIIIIIIIIIIIIIIIIIIIIIIIIIIIIIIIIIIIIIIIIIIIIIIIIIIIIIIIIIIIIIIIIIIIIIIIIIIIIIIIIIIIIIIIIIIIIIIIIIIIIIIIIII

PROJECT DESCRIPTION & DESIGN STRATEGY:

When you leave design school and look for work with your portfolio of fictitious student projects, half of your interviewers will pause to tell you that in the "real world" you'll never have the opportunity to design wine packaging—much less packaging themed after one of your favorite movies. Unless, of course, you get a job at Helms Workshop, and then have the chance to design for Alamo Drafthouse Cinemas.

In looking at developing an identity for Alamo's in-house branded wines, Helms Workshop decided that it would be impossible to sum up everything that makes the Alamo unique in a single packaging system. Instead, they opted to redesign the wine each year,

based on a film that aligns with the brand. Alamo's 2012 offering is two wines inspired by The Princess Bride, in honor of the twenty-fifth anniversary of the film. As fans will recognize, "The Bottle of Wits" is derived from the iconic "battle of wits" scene between Westley and Vizzini. Movie dialogue also inspired the varietal names: "Inconceivable Cab" and "As You Wish White."

TIP

Cult classic movies, childhood nostalgia, and pop culture are great sources for utilizing humor and wit in your packaging design. Just remember to choose references that have pretty broad appeal. Otherwise your package will be like Dennis Miller on Monday Night Football. (Too obscure? Case in point, friends.)

HUSTLER
The Joy Lin, USA

PROJECT DESCRIPTION & DESIGN STRATEGY:

The Hustler redesign celebrates the erotic duality of masculinity and femininity. Products are featured in a twofold nature, playing with relation, contrast, movement, and penetration. With the idea of two becoming one, Hustler shifts its focus toward couples, thus expanding its market and reestablishing itself as a leader in the sex industry.

TIP

Working with the subject of sex, which is often considered taboo, was initially a challenge. The Joy Lin created packaging that is sexy without being overtly raunchy. That mind-set helped them develop a beautiful design with a subliminal logo, subtle wording, and erotic forms that are not obvious at a first glance and are very sexy at a second glance.

YOU SMELL

Megan Cummins and Aaron Heth, USA

PROJECT DESCRIPTION & DESIGN STRATEGY:

The goal of this packaging was to create a conversation starter around each bath product from You Smell. The witty name, cheeky copy, candy-colored hues, and soap fragrances entice the audience to touch, smell, and talk about these bath and beauty products. Vintage-inspired woodcut illustrations, elegant typography, and ornate flourishes create a fun and charming personality for a brand that feels handmade.

LESSONS LEARNED ALONG THE WAY:

Experiment with die lines and paper weights. Test each weight, as measurements can change with each paper's thickness.

Designer Megan Cummins says: "You don't want to end up with thousands of boxes in slightly the wrong size, or tabs that won't close."

Design should be experiential just like humor. Every paper flap, tab, and block of copy works together to tell a story as it's revealed. Surprise and delight your audience with clever illustrations or phrases strategically placed in your packaging.

LIKE
SWEET
SEDUCTION
Thanks to us!

Let's face it: people like people who smell good, and sometimes this can be a daunting task. Allow us to help. You Smell® has handcrafted you the finest soap, rich in softening shea butter and moisturizing olive oil. This all-natural soap will cleanse the body and ease the soul. Just lather and wash your way to happiness.

Warning: for external use only. Do not ingest soap. That would be ridiculous. Avoid contact with eyes.

Formulated in the US by You Smell, LLC. Made in China. Call 415.244.2419 www.YouSmellSoap.com

INGREDIENTS: SODIUM PALMATE, SODIUM PALM KERNELATE, AQUA (WATER), SHEA BUTTER OIL, OLEA EUROPAEA (OLIVE) FRUIT OIL, PARFUM (FRAGRANCE), GLYCERIN, SODIUM CHLORIDE, SODIUM HYDROSULFITE, TETRASODIUM EDTA, CI 16255 (COLOR), GENERAL STATE OF HAPPINESS, COPIOUS AMOUNTS OF COMPLIMENTS

Made with Shea Butter and Olive Oil

All Natural Product. No Parabens. No Phthalates.

TABULA RASA
YOU SMELL
ALL NATURAL GOODNESS

Chapter 13

PACKAGING FOR KIDS

WORK AND PLAY. FUN FOR ALL. Packaging for kids' products is about as much fun as you can have. Following our belief that to best understand and define a design direction, you need to relate (or become) that person, this is an opportunity to be a kid again.

•••

We certainly appreciate the austere refinement of designing for luxury brands, but often wish that a super-soaker client would come our way. With even just a mention of super soaker, everyone reading this probably has a mental image of what the packaging looks like. Taken one step further, how about introducing squirt guns for toddlers, senior citizens, or even lower-volume versions for office use? While we certainly don't condone violence in any form, a squirt gun could be brought to market with a message of positivity when packaged appropriately. By focusing on fun, age-appropriateness, and orienting the aesthetics to the emotional outcome of a squirt-gun fight (hint: it's happiness and laughter), the package could really help sell product, even to new audiences.

While not exactly kid-specific, we would be remiss not to mention how we like to orient ourselves when considering a design solution. Rather than focus on the obvious—this is a squirt gun, this is for kids, we should use very bright colors and more than one exclamation mark—we instead choose to focus on the most emotional outcome of the product's intended use. This is a very important mental state to achieve because this is where your package design will connect with the most likely consumer. No matter what you design, if you appeal to the emotions of your audience in a way that feels honest and sincere, people will develop a bond with your brand. Legacy brands are built this way. Coke doesn't sell sugar water, McDonald's doesn't sell fried potatoes, and Lego sure as hell doesn't sell little plastic bricks. Everyone sells experiences, and to be successful, an experience must tap emotion.

Enough heavy stuff. One important element to consider when designing for children is the physical difference in their bodies. What may feel comfortable in your hand may be unwieldy in the hands of a child. Likewise, while we are not advocates of dumbing things down, you will be competing for a very, very short attention span. Keep your imagery specific and with an exaggerated scale, your messaging direct, and your emotional appeal on point. One other tip is that children love to discover new ways to amuse themselves. In essence, constant amusement (educational or otherwise) is what defines our dream-scenario childhood. Turning a used raisin box into a quick toy with a few folds is not about the toy, it is about the experience of transformation and discovery. It is

EROSKI DIAPERS

Supperstudio, Spain

PROJECT DESCRIPTION & DESIGN STRATEGY:

In order to break from the traditional imagery seen on diaper packaging—cute, crawling, happy babies—Supperstudio decided instead to craft imagery that spoke directly to the end consumers, those cute, crawling, happy babies. They started by establishing a color that would differentiate them from the competition and then began creating images that would appeal to young ones, and therefore their parents. Elephants, giraffes, ducks, cows, and hippos became the identifying characters that help make this product line unique and memorable.

TIP

Be wary of a trend that falls into the "everybody's doing it" category. While there might be good reason so many of the competitors chose a certain path (you'll have a very happy baby if you choose these diapers), it's also the perfect chance to catch a consumer's eye by doing the exact opposite.

also brilliant and hits on one of the most important elements of childhood: snack time. If you can channel your creativity into clever packaging like this, you won't just be loved by kids everywhere, you'll be rich.

We discuss quite a bit about how packaging for the youth market is about captivating the imaginations of children. That stated, we would be remiss not to point out that the most likely purchaser is an adult. Recognizing this, make sure your copy has a second level to any humor and your typography has a sophistication that says more than just "fun product," but "quality company." Conveying quality is key to converting adult consumers because children's products carry the weight of responsibility and reflect parenting judgment. All heaviness aside, the best packages—like the best Disney movies—convey two separate story lines aimed at amusing the children, entertaining the adults, and occasionally employing a carefully crafted double entendre.

Quickly, a few no-nos that will earn you a time-out (sorry, we absolutely could not resist). Never speak down to children. They most likely have been born into the Internet era, and their knowledge

base is best judged in dog years. If your package contains a dinosaur replica, do not be afraid to go all paleontologist with your copy. If you are packaging a product with a deep brand history (think SpongeBob, Barney, Harry Potter, etc.), recognize that your audience likely has an encyclopedic knowledge of every bit of ephemera ever produced. Use that to your advantage and don't worry about them "getting it." If they don't immediately recognize a reference, it will be Googled in seconds. Beyond not speaking down to an audience, a good rule of thumb is to always aim for a grade or two above the target demographic. Until you hit the legal drinking age for alcohol, age appropriation will always skew higher. What we would give to have those days back.

STAFIDENIOS
Matadog Design, Greece

IIIIIIIIIIIIIIIIIIIIIIIIIIIIIIIIIIIIIIIIIIIIIIIIIIIIIIIIIIIIIIIIII

PROJECT DESCRIPTION & DESIGN STRATEGY:

Stafidenios is a raisin product packed for kids and made in Greece. The packaging dimensions are designed to fit into a kid's cupped hand. Research in a world market study showed that all raisin packaging had the same motif. An opportunity in the consumption chain for extended packaging use was then identified. The paper is reusable—kids can make paper toys out of the inside of the box. It's an added gift to the buyer and still adheres to the production budget. The innovated packaging has been trademarked.

TIP

Matadog Design encountered and solved many technical challenges in paper, artwork, and die-cutting due to the product size. To do so, they had to explore how paper toys were made and identify the pros and cons of the construction process. One of the major disadvantages found was the need for glue and blade cutters. Not all families have time to acquire those tools when providing a quick snack for children. Plus, the effort and complexity made that route inconvenient for the family. The final design requires no additional tools, just cleverly placed tabs and die-cuts.

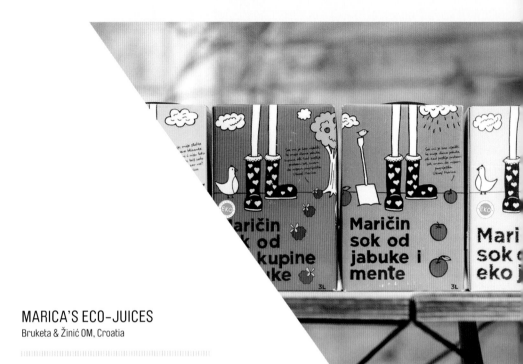

MARICA'S ECO-JUICES
Bruketa & Žinić OM, Croatia

PROJECT DESCRIPTION & DESIGN STRATEGY:

Marica's Eco-Juices are produced by Marica Jug on her family farm, just outside of Našice, Croatia. The bag-in-box packaging was conceived and designed by Bruketa & Žinić OM. The juice is made from organically grown fruit, without any additives, except a lot of love. It is based on cold-pressed apple juice, with a range of interesting flavors, such as elderberry, mint, blackberry, and pure sour cherry juice. To bring the story behind these juices closer to consumers, illustrations of a day in the life of Marica are used on the packaging. Examples include Marica's feet in work boots, her shovels, baskets filled with fruit, fruit trees, birds, and other helpful garden animals. Marica also wrote a short letter about her farm and her juices on the packaging.

Chapter 14
ALCOHOL, SPIRITS, WINE, + BEER

ELEVATED SPIRITS. Who doesn't love beer, wine, spirits, and all of the wonderful types of adult beverages? Package designers, that's who. While the notion of working in such a fun industry is delightful, the reality is that the category is packed with great design, and setting yourself apart while building a brand is extremely difficult. But if you relish a challenge—and we certainly do—this is the time to flex your creativity.

• • •

When a new alcoholic beverage launches, the packaging must carry the entire brand and convey such a strong description of flavor profile, purpose, or message that a potential consumer is likely to at least pick up the bottle to find out a little more. Once someone picks up a package, the battle for conversion is almost won.

So how do you pique someone's interest in a crowded marketplace? This is a loaded question, but we can address it by dissecting the first sentence of this paragraph. Is the beverage in question a unique taste profile compared to the rest of the marketplace? Gin, for example, has a wide range of styles, but nothing so redefined what a gin could be as much as the cucumber-inspired Hendricks Gin. While they cleverly didn't put an illustration of a cucumber on the label, they address the uniqueness of the taste in the primary copy.

Is the drink in question a stand-alone, or is it meant to be mixed with others? Perhaps the best example of a modern-day mixer owning an audience is St. Germain. St. Germain has an arguably fictitious origin and ingredient list, is not a stand-alone drink, has a very high price point given the nature of manufacture and category, yet is so ubiquitous in the back bars of high-end cocktail lounges that it is often referred to as "bartender's ketchup." To begin, they created the messaging that this was an essential component in complex cocktail mixology. Second, they created a unique bottle that speaks to the faux French heritage and price point. Finally, they co-pack limited editions with a mixing cup, stir stick, and recipes. We can only speculate on the cost of the liquid, but it is clear that the profit margin is high enough to merit spending this kind of money on packaging and story line. It is also clear that this type of synergy is successful.

On a more practical scale was the work that we were fortunate to do with Death's Door Spirits. Theirs was a unique problem because the bottle production budget could never compete with the largest brands, but the story line and liquid were every bit as good as the largest players in the marketplace. The million-dollar question became how can we punch above our weight and compete? The answer was to create a sense of origin right there on the label while planting key messaging points with the people who were in the market sampling the product. Death's Door Passage is a dangerous waterway between mainland Wisconsin and Washington Island, where the raw goods to make the spirits are grown. Using a map and apothecary-inspired typography helped remove the brand from its previous pirate-focused identity while establishing that this product was made in a real place and benefited from a maritime climate. The inspirational story behind the brand and the families who produce it is another compelling reason for consumers to purchase Death's Door over the competition. After all, when ordering a cocktail, would you rather send five dollars to a multinational conglomerate or two farmers in Wisconsin? Throw in that the product was included in the Best Spirits by Wine & Spirits and you have the origin of Death's Door Spirits' amazing journey to where they sit today: leading the American craft spirit revolution. *See the Death's Door case study on page 16.*

> **TIP**
>
> *Know the mandatory TTB (www.ttb. gov) rules and regulations. They dictate sizing and required information for alcohol.*

CHAVA RUM
Archrival/Dachis Group, USA

||||||||||||||||||||||||||||||||||||||||||||||||||||||||||||||||||||||||||

PROJECT DESCRIPTION & DESIGN STRATEGY:

Chava Rum is a new premium craft rum
made with the finest local ingredients in the
Midwest. The objective was to design a bottle
that had a hand-grifted feel while establishing
a high-end look on the shelf. The challenge for
this project was to help a new and relatively
small company tap a larger market with a
proportional budget that national brands have.

TIP

*To save money on production, the final design
consisted of a one-color screenprint on the bottle and
two die-cut labels that appear to overlap.*

TIP

Create unexpected design solutions by thinking about how a consumer will interact with packaging. The Bitter Sisters packaging contains imagery of two sisters on the back panel; one is right side up and appears angry, while the other is upside down and smiling. When poured, the orientation of the two sisters is reversed.

BITTER SISTERS
COCKTAIL MIXERS
Device Creative Collaborative, USA

PROJECT DESCRIPTION & DESIGN STRATEGY:

Winston-Salem area bar Single Brothers concocted these tasty bitters. Originally sipped as a health tonic in the 1800s, bitters were eventually mingled with more powerful beverages to become cocktails. The design aesthetic is a throwback to that bygone era, from the brown medicine bottle to the ornate embellishments and flourishes, elaborate type work, and letterpress printing. The name Bitter Sisters is a play on words, referencing the product and brand story.

JOHNNIE WALKER
NEW ZEALAND LIMITED EDITION
The Creative Method, Australia

PROJECT DESCRIPTION & DESIGN STRATEGY:

The brief was to create packaging for Johnnie Walker to be sold in New Zealand during and after the Rugby World Cup. It also had to double as a pack that would be purchased by Kiwis to help raise funds for the Christchurch earthquake appeal. The approach was to be non-rugby-specific by taking the silver fern icon and integrating it into the Johnnie Walker striding man. It was simple, stood out, and was crafted in such a way that it reflected the quality and craftsmanship of the liquid. Sales increased significantly, and a similar project has been undertaken for the Thailand marketplace.

JOHNNIE WALKER

BLACK LABEL

Blended Scotch Whisky

PRODUCT OF SCOTLAND

KIRK AND SWEENEY RUM

Studio 32 North, USA

|||||||||||||||||||||||||||||||||||||||||||||||||||||||||||||||||||||

PROJECT DESCRIPTION & DESIGN STRATEGY:

Kirk and Sweeney was a wooden schooner, best known for smuggling rum from the Caribbean to the Northeast during the early years of Prohibition. The bottle and the raised cork were inspired by the elegantly squat eighteenth-century onion bottles, which typically contained rum. Playing off the concept of global navigation, an antique nautical map of the main rum-smuggling route is silkscreened around the circumference of the bottle. The neck features custom hand-numbering, which speaks to the rare and precious nature of the cargo. Along with the ornate logo, the photo of the ship, and the safety seal printed to look like nautical brass, the design serves as a reminder of the risk so many were willing to take for a taste of quality Caribbean rum during the 1920s.

TIP

Printing on a variety of surfaces can be difficult. Glass, paper, foil, cork, and corrugated material (for the shipper) offer their own unique processes—and then trying to match colors between them was virtually impossible. Designer Sallie Reynolds Allen says: "We overcame this with a design process that methodically put one step in front of the other, allowing us to make color adjustments as we went. While it seemed like we were losing some control, we learned to be more flexible in our color choices, which ultimately allowed for more creativity."

TIP

Cat Spinelli from The Creative Method says, "The big lesson when ordering shipper cartons is that the designer should always confirm that they are the correct size for the bottles. In the case of BYO we purchased a whole lot of shippers, and they would not fit a full complement of bottles."

BYO WINE
The Creative Method, Australia

PROJECT DESCRIPTION & DESIGN STRATEGY:

The Creative Method created this unique packaging as Christmas gifts for clients and for new business introductions. It reminded the recipient of who the bottle was from and the long hours agency designers put into their work. It featured the entire staff and reflected creativity and sense of humor. Each of the 5,000 labels was based on a staff member. They included a number of facial features, and the client is encouraged to BYO—Build Your Own. The wine and the label were the perfect substitute for when the real thing cannot be there.

TIN MAN BREWING CO. BEER

Melodic Virtue/Wagner Design, USA

PROJECT DESCRIPTION & DESIGN STRATEGY:

Tin Man Brewing Co. is a new microbrewery in Evansville, Indiana. They had the typical client challenge to differentiate their product from competitors. The tin man concept was carried through in the vintage oil aesthetic and copy. Unlike competitors that have artwork completely covering the can, Tin Man cans avoid printing and expose the aluminum whenever possible.

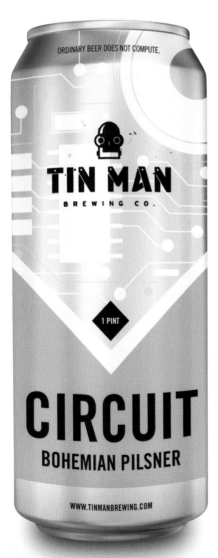

STINA

Brandoctor & Bruketa & Žinić, Croatia

||||||||||||||||||||||||||||||||||||||||||||||||||||||||||||||||

PROJECT DESCRIPTION & DESIGN STRATEGY:

Stina wine comes from the Adriatic island of
Brac, known for white stone and beautiful
nature. It is a source of inspiration to many
sculptors, painters, and novelists. The wine
label is intentionally left blank, encouraging
the buyer to create a masterpiece from
spilled wine on the white, rocklike surface.

TIP

The original black matte capsule design changed to accommodate constraints from this Croatian vendor. Every vendor is different, so be sure to test foils and embossing from various vendors to recognize their capabilities and limitations.

THE KILLER PROSECCO

TypeSpace, Australia

|||||||||||||||||||||||||||||||||||||||||||||||||||||||||||||||||||||||||||||||||||

PROJECT DESCRIPTION & DESIGN STRATEGY:

Inspired by Italian fashion and film of the
1940s and 1950s, The Killer brand conveys
mystery, intrigue, and sensuality. The Killer
Prosecco, the newest bottle in the series,
carries through the brand elements,
including the fishnet capsule to the
sparkling wine category.

TIP

*his bottle was designed by TypeSpace, in Australia, but
*oduced with Italian vendors. Clear instructions were given to
*e vendors, enabling the overseas process to run smoothly and
*inimize production errors. When in doubt, overexplain what
ur intentions are and what you expect for the final product.

Chapter 15

MAKE IT GIFTABLE

GIFTED CHILDREN. Just like with children, we're not supposed to have favorite projects (or clients). But what designer doesn't love the project that comes along with that extra budget for special printing and production? Often these projects fall into the "giftable" category—those packages that get extra-special treatment because they are likely to be given as gifts.

• • •

The packaging becomes even more critical in these cases, and it's often an opportunity to use unique printing techniques or unusual substrates. And consider this: gift package projects are also likely to carry a lot of emotional baggage for the purchaser.

Does emotional baggage sound like too heavy a term? Consider this: in essence, a gift represents the gift giver and creates an environment whereupon the recipient will judge the giver based on what was given. Years ago we worked with a theater company to help determine the appropriateness of specific media types— stay with us, this is going somewhere. What we accidentally discovered is that rarely do people go to the theater by themselves, and the act of inviting another couple as guests (consider this the "gift" of tickets) allowed those guests to judge their friends based on the quality of the show they were invited to see. The interesting element to this is that a negative experience discouraged further interaction not just with the offending gift givers, but with theater itself. The lesson to be learned is that while the surface of gift giving is goodwill, the quality of the gift, or at least the perceived quality, is roughly equivalent to the relationship between giver and receiver. Emotional baggage, indeed.

So how do you create memorable, high-quality, and emotional packaging decisions? Of course, the usual suspects apply here: great typography, personality in messaging, and contemporary color palettes. But there is one element that conveys so much more, and that element is tactility. By tactility we mean more than just surface treatments, but also weight and shape.

We deal with a lot of interior design firms at Grip, and they all say the same thing: spend money on things that people touch. Door handles should be heavy and latch firmly, toilet levers should be tight, and drawer pulls should not have cheap or plastic finishes. When you think about it, how many things do you really touch, versus how many do you look at? You get the point—tactility counts. It's why car commercials all have heavily enhanced "thuds" when the door shuts. The sound implies weight, and that in turn implies quality.

When we were working with Death's Door Spirits and discussing the price-to-market, it became obvious that as a super-premium product at super-premium pricing, we were not going to get a lot of college-age buyers. More likely, this would be for connoisseurs and gift buyers. Responding to this, we utilized a restrained color palette, set the type in a manner not often found in the category (pre-Prohibition-inspired apothecary), and made sure the bottle was the clearest glass, with very few seams, and heavy for its size.

One final example of how important the giftable nature of a product can be: How many of you can remember the last time you thought of ordering a drink with Crown Royal Whiskey? Most likely very few. But there you are, standing in the liquor-store aisle looking for a last-minute gift for Grandpa and there it is, just staring at you. The. Stupid. Bag. Something takes over, and your mind races with the elegance of presenting Pops with not just another bottle of booze, but one that comes in a cloth bag. We would love to keep saying "that stupid bag" (because, come on, it *is* pretty ugly), but that bag is one of the smartest marketing tools ever created for Crown Royal, and our hunch is that a few of you have laundry quarters in one at this very moment. That stu--, er, smartly utilized bag not only sold more bottles of booze, it has also outlived the product itself.

The trend of co-packing is now more widespread than ever, and just one glance down the spirits aisle during the holiday season will prove that not only is it popular, but it works. Keep this in mind and do not hesitate to suggest a co-pack to clients when you think that two products can sell more together than independently. That, after all, will be just one more package you get to design.

MAISON DANDOY BAKERY
Base Design, Belgium

PROJECT DESCRIPTION & DESIGN STRATEGY:

Founded in 1829, Dandoy is a traditional Brussels bakery that prides itself on a rich heritage of *savoir faire* and artisanal craftsmanship. A playful take on a long-established historical legacy, the new Maison Dandoy brand and packaging are built from a graphic toolbox that consists simply of a logo, elegant typography, limited illustrations, and a streamlined color palette of just black, white, and gold. Beautifully structured but simple packaging was designed to reduce waste and still catch the eye and make for a lovely gift.

SOFI BATH BOMBS
Popular Bruketa & Žinić, Serbia

PROJECT DESCRIPTION & DESIGN STRATEGY:

Sofi is a small family production of organic
handmade cosmetics from Serbia. The idea
behind the packaging of their Sofi Bath Bombs
was to emphasize the manual production and
the quality of the resources, as well as of the
final products. The materials utilized in the
packaging help tell this story, and the slightly
distressed aesthetic quality of the printing in
contrast with the gold-foil stamp makes the
package distinctive and perfect for gifting.
Each bath bomb appears to be so lovingly
packaged, it implies the pampering to come
when the consumer uses the product.

TIP

Knowing the market is critical to creating a package that stands out. The dramatic typographic treatments on these Sofi packages are very distinctive in the Serbian market, where oversized and type-driven solutions are uncommon.

HOLY WATER
The Creative Method, Australia

PROJECT DESCRIPTION & DESIGN STRATEGY:

This gift that The Creative Method gave to clients had three critical goals: remind clients of TCM's ability to think differently; make an immediate impact as a memorable and unique gift; invite clients to the end-of-year party. In other words, this single wine bottle had to be a gift clients would love, a portfolio piece, and double as a party invitation to boot (a tall order for any project). This was all accomplished with a sense of humor and surprising, fun illustrations. Each staff member was photographed and then brought to life in a traditional horror-book style. The story follows the characters' experimentation with Holy Water and the catastrophic results. Each bottle contains two "pages" from the story, and there are six in the set. This is a great way to intrigue customers and create desire to collect them all.

CONFECTION OVEN® CHOCOLATE SEA SALT CARAMELS & FRENCH MACAROONS

KLS Graphic Design, USA

PROJECT DESCRIPTION & DESIGN STRATEGY:

Designed for a boutique bakery in San Diego, the goal was to create a unique line of packaging that represented their handcrafted confections and attention to detail. The color palette is simple and classic, as is the package itself: a kraft brown tube with paper caps for the caramels and a matchbox-style, kraft brown box for the macaroons. They are branded with understated but elegant black-and-white labels—a very cost-effective solution without losing the loveliness of these coveted treats.

TIP

Functionality doesn't have to be ugly. Each macaroon box was embellished with a silver eyelet and a satin pull-string ribbon with the company's logo. The ribbon does indeed help with ease of use (getting to those delicious macaroons faster), but it also adds to the charm and stylishness of the package.

CHOCO CARDS

Voov Ltd., Hungary

PROJECT DESCRIPTION & DESIGN STRATEGY:

The idea behind Choco Cards is simple: give chocolate and a postcard in one box as a new—and more delicious—alternative to traditional greeting cards.

The chocolate box is designed to encase a postcard that is slipped into the lid, and the message written on the back is revealed upon opening the box. The recipient sees the richly adorned chocolate together with a heartwarming note from the sender. Each element of the gift is selected by the user: the box, the postcard, the personal message, and even the chocolate and ingredients used to make the candy housed inside. The goal was to craft a lovely, personal experience for the gift giver and recipient.

Chapter 16
END CAP

RESOURCES. For all new packaging projects, we have two kickoff meetings with the client. The first pertains to the goals of the project and the second deals with production, planning, timing, and budget. Here are a few lists you can use to plan your next packaging project.

• • •

PACKAGING PROJECT KICKOFF MEETING QUESTIONS

QUESTIONS FOR THE CLIENT.

☐ What is your story?

☐ What is the product and concept?

☐ Will the product be one-off or will it be required to work in a system? (If there is a system, is there a clear understanding of the company vs. product names?)

☐ What are the goals, objectives, and directives of the project?

☐ Who is the audience?

☐ What companies or products are the direct and indirect competitors?

☐ What is the time frame? Are there any milestones or events that are driving deadlines? If so, what are they and when?

☐ Is the product the first of its kind on the market? If so, what education does the buyer need?

☐ If the project is a refresh, what problems need to be solved? Is there anything that should be incorporated from the old package to the new?

☐ Where is the content coming from? (Who will provide the messaging, and is there existing artwork or logos that need to be considered?)

☐ Who are the decision makers?

☐ Is the product still in development, and are there samples available?

QUESTIONS FOR THE STUDIO.

☐ What items are on the contract? (e.g., product and system naming, messaging, identity, primary packaging, secondary packaging)

☐ How many hours are allotted to this project?

☐ Identify the assigned designer, writer, photographer, project manager, etc. as well as establish who is responsible for each task within the project.

☐ When are the internal and client deadlines?

☐ Who will create or collect the content and assets?

☐ Will the product be photographed, and if so, by whom?

PACKAGING PRODUCTION MEETING QUESTIONS

☐ What is the production budget?

☐ Is the design studio in charge of production, or is the client tasked with that (and billed directly by the vendor)?

☐ What quantities are needed (or required) for manufacturing?

☐ Is there a vendor already selected?

☐ What are the vendor capabilities?

☐ Is any part of the product or packaging manufactured or produced overseas? If so, are transportation and shipping times accounted for in the timeline? Who is overseeing that process?

☐ If a packaging system needs to be created, what are the initial agreed-upon products?

☐ Are custom bottles or containers going to be created? If so, how long will it take to produce the needed quantity?

☐ Is there an interim solution if the custom containers cannot be created?

☐ Does the overall production schedule align with the initial time frame? If not, alert the client, present an alternative solution, or revise the schedule.

☐ If the product is food, when will the nutrition facts be finalized?

WHAT WOULD YOU THINK IF WE SANG OUT OF TUNE?

Honestly, the single greatest part of writing this book has been the relationships we have with all of the contributors, editors, and sources we leaned on for help. Some people we knew, some we didn't, but all are now family. We once listened to a pastor at a big rally here in town whip the crowd into a frenzy with the proclamation that, "It takes teamwork to make the dream work," and never have we believed it more than with this book. Thank you all for your role in our dream.

It would be easy to consider some of the case studies in this book "proprietary" or perhaps even too revealing of internal processes that are used to consistently maintain quality. That so many of you decided to help us and the design community by sharing your knowledge is truly humbling. If nothing else, consider your karma bank loaded.

Our profession has undergone radical change in the past two decades, and keeping up with the new skills required for success is a daunting proposition. It is, however, a challenge made easier by replacing interindustry competition with interindustry cooperation. The rapid changes that create the need for new skills also create the opportunity for new revenue streams and compensation structures. We propose that by working together, we have more to gain than by forcing ourselves apart by withholding best practices. At the end of the day, we all enjoy the respect afforded our industry by the individuals and companies that practice the craft at the highest levels. Sharing that knowledge is the key to moving forward. Thanks to all of you, who shared so much with us. Feel free to stop by the studio. The first seven drinks are on us.

Established in 1999, Grip has over a decade of strategic design experience. Servicing clients in a range of industries, our primary goal with every project is to achieve quantifiable results. Through the years this disciplined approach has honed our research skills and maximized the return potential of our clients. Our design team leaders have a breadth of knowledge that spans both online and printed environments. As a full-service creative agency, we constantly strive to add the highest-value communication vehicles to our evolving skill set. That noted, perhaps the most telling statistic about our storied history is that we still work with our very first client.

A NEW MODEL AGENCY. We collaborate and drive innovation by looking at a client's situation and imagining the possibilities from many angles, a 3D approach to problem solving, truly bringing an idea to life. It's the next level of branding and positioning that stems from shared values with our clients and ultimately results in business growth and evolution. As a New Model Agency, we help our clients create new methods to grow their business, while they are occupied with running their business. Often this employs line extensions or new distribution models, but also takes form in advanced social media strategy and unique merchandising solutions. There is no singular fix, only the most effective blend.

Grip®

1128 N. ASHLAND AVENUE, CHICAGO, IL 60622
312-906-8020 / GRIPDESIGN.COM
TWITTER @HELLOGRIP
FACEBOOK.COM/GRIPDESIGN